Into the Spotlight

D1446035

PROJECT SPONSORS

Missouri Center for the Book
Western Historical Manuscript Collection, University
of Missouri–Columbia

SPECIAL THANKS

Dr. Randy McGuire, Pius XII Memorial Library,
Saint Louis University
Richard A. Martin, Jr., who is carrying on the legend
of his aunt, Josephine Baker, in St. Louis
Christine Montgomery, Photographic Specialist, State
Historical Society of Columbia
Harry S. Truman Library, Independence
Western Historical Manuscript Collection, St. Louis
and others who have made this book possible

MISSOURI HERITAGE READERS
General Editor, Rebecca B. Schroeder

Each Missouri Heritage Reader explores a particular aspect of the state's rich cultural heritage. Focusing on people, places, historical events, and the details of daily life, these books illustrate the ways in which people from all parts of the world contributed to the development of the state and the region. The books incorporate documentary and oral history, folklore, and informal literature in a way that makes these resources accessible to all Missourians.

Intended primarily for adult new readers, these books will also be invaluable to readers of all ages interested in the cultural and social history of Missouri.

OTHER BOOKS IN THE SERIES

Into the Spotlight

FOUR

MISSOURI WOMEN

———◆———

Margot Ford McMillen

and

Heather Roberson

UNIVERSITY OF MISSOURI PRESS

COLUMBIA AND LONDON

Copyright © 2004 by
The Curators of the University of Missouri
University of Missouri Press, Columbia, Missouri 65201
Printed and bound in the United States of America
All rights reserved
5 4 3 2 1   08 07 06 05 04

Library of Congress Cataloging-in-Publication Data

McMillen, Margot Ford.
   Into the spotlight : four Missouri women / Margot Ford McMillen and
Heather Roberson.
        p. cm. — (Missouri heritage readers)
Includes bibliographical references and index.
   ISBN 0-8262-1556-4 (alk. paper)
   1. Sacred Sun, ca. 1809–1835 or 6. 2. Blair, Emily Newell, b. 1877. 3.
Baker, Josephine, 1906–1975. 4. Truman, Bess Wallace. 5. Women—
Missouri—Biography. 6. Missouri—Biography. I. Roberson, Heather. II.
Title. III. Series.
   CT3262.M8M38 2004
   920.72'09778—dc22

                                                              2004016159

∞™ This paper meets the requirements of the
American National Standard for Permanence of Paper
for Printed Library Materials, Z39.48, 1984.

Designer: Stephanie Foley
Typesetter: Foley Design
Cover design: Kristie Lee
Printer and binder: Thomson-Shore, Inc.
Typefaces: Dorchester Script and Garamond

To Becky, a mentor and friend whose courage always turns into encouragement

Contents

Preface

One isn't necessarily born with courage, but one is
born with potential. Without courage, we cannot
practice any other virtue with consistency. We can't
be kind, true, merciful, generous or honest.

—Maya Angelou

Each of us has a unique place in history. We may have been
born in peacetime or during a time of war. We may find
that those around us are rich or poor, generous or fearful.
Even our parents—those closest to us—may be kind and con-
fident or unsympathetic.

When life hands us a challenge, the way we cope with the
situation depends in great part on the models we find; by reading biographies of others, we can increase the number and
types of examples to follow. In our earlier book, *Called to
Courage: Four Women in Missouri History,* published by the
University of Missouri Press in 2002, we explored the lives of
four remarkable women whose experiences spanned two centuries. Their courage pushed them to lives of sacrifice and
heroism that can inspire and encourage others.

Ignon Ouaconisen, or "Françoise of the Missouri Nation,"
traveled to France in 1725 with the explorer Etienne de
Bourgmont and leaders of the Missouri, Osage, and other
tribes; Olive Vanbibber Boone immigrated to the Louisiana

Territory with her husband, Nathan, in 1799, cared for her father-in-law, Daniel Boone, during his last days, and managed their home during Nathan's long absences; Martha Jane Chisley Tolton, brought to Missouri as a slave, escaped to Illinois with her young children during the Civil War and saw that her son Augustine was educated for the priesthood; Nell Donnelly Reed, daughter of an Irish immigrant, built a large manufacturing business in Kansas City, providing opportunities for many women and achieving a success and high profile that brought her new challenges.

In this volume, four new biographies demonstrate how women of different backgrounds gained positions of prominence—whether through dedicated effort or through chance—and used their unique skills to empower themselves and others. The effects of these remarkable lives still touch us today, and they inspire us to push ourselves beyond the boundaries society has set.

Sacred Sun, also called Mohongo, was a Native American of the Osage tribe. In 1827, she journeyed to Europe with a group of six prominent Osage and a French promoter at a time when her people had lost their land in Missouri, their sacred places, and many of their traditions. Sacred Sun and her fellow travelers were received as celebrities but later fell out of favor and wandered friendless throughout Europe. After experiencing harrowing adventures, even giving birth to twin daughters, Sacred Sun returned with her fellow travelers to the Osage tribe, which had been moved to Oklahoma and was still struggling to survive.

Almost a century later, Emily Newell Blair was born into a successful southwest Missouri family. Raised by parents who encouraged her to get an education and expand her skills in writing and speaking, she had the talents and social position that enabled her to be an effective public leader. She used her opportunities and abilities to help push the United States to extend the vote to women.

Another remarkable woman, Josephine Baker, grew up in segregated, turn-of-the-century St. Louis, a society that judged the worth of each person according to color. Her mixed ethnic background meant that she fit in neither with her own black family nor with white society, and it was largely this racial injustice that pushed her to hone her own daring performance style so that she could prove to the world that she and other women of color could excel and make important contributions to society. She became a theater and dance star, toured Europe, served as a spy during World War II, and was a fervent civil rights and antiracism activist.

The subject of our final essay grew up in one of Missouri's most prominent families and married a neighborhood boy who was considered unacceptable by her mother. The young couple struggled for several years to make ends meet as he failed in one enterprise after another—until they eventually found their place in politics. Bess Truman, called "the Boss" by her husband, President Harry S. Truman, worked side by side with him, edited his speeches, and advised and guided him through innumerable crises during and after World War II, before they gratefully retired to their family home back in Missouri.

We are indebted to many researchers, readers, and guides who helped us find these stories and context. Rebecca Schroeder, the editor of Missouri Heritage Series, always provided encouragement and insisted that each essay be much better than we ever imagined.

The research staffs of the State Historical Society of Missouri, the Western Historical Manuscripts Collection, the Truman Library, the Missouri Historical Society, the Powers Museum, and Westminster College provided support above and beyond the call of duty and, as always, our final reader, Howard Marshall, provided fresh eyes and new insights as the manuscripts approached completion.

Into the Spotlight

Sacred Sun

There is an Osage woman & her child at William's.
The Secretary agrees if you will paint her & introduce
the head of her child for 20$ to have her painted.

—Memo from Thomas McKenney, U.S. Superintendent
of Indian Affairs, to Charles Bird King, artist, 1830

*B*orn around 1809, Sacred Sun—also called Mohongo—
was part of the last Osage generation to experience traditional life in the tribal homeland, an area that included much
of today's state of Missouri. In 1827 Sacred Sun was one of six
Osage—four men and two women—who journeyed to France
with a French-born entrepreneur. In Europe, the Osage travelers became a unique attraction, greeted with great curiosity
and wild enthusiasm. Journalists in Europe and the United
States followed their travels. Later, the Osage still drew attention from the press when they were, sadly, wandering in
Europe abandoned and impoverished. The news reports have
become major sources of information about the lives of Sacred
Sun and the others in the group.

For the most part, Osage history, and that of other Native
Americans, passed orally from generation to generation. As
elders died, many histories were lost; this is especially true for
the lives and stories of women, because most travelers did not
try to interview them. Although women were the caregivers,

1

food producers, and even at times peacemakers of their tribes, historians and journalists generally only noted that women worked hard, believing their roles were not worthy of detailed discussion. Thus most recorded history is about the men's realm—the history of battles and of hunting lands acquired and lost. By reconstructing the lives of women like Sacred Sun, we gain a more complete understanding of the cultures and events in our region long before Missouri became a state.

Because of her celebrity, we know some details about Sacred Sun, but there are still many unanswered questions. Were these Osage travelers in full control of their journey? Were they seeking the help of the French after losing their land to Americans? Or were they innocents, under the spell of a clever businessman? Some of the answers will never be known.

The first home for the Osage in Missouri, according to Osage tradition, was at the Place-of-the-Many-Swans, called by the French Marais des Cygnes, in present-day Vernon County on the river Americans later called the Osage. The people built their villages on riverbanks in locations near both forests and prairies. Each ecosystem provided different wild game and plants—for instance, the forests provided bear and deer, while the prairies held the buffalo—and the waterways provided beaver and fish. The rivers also served as a means of transportation for trading. Longhouses sheltered the families in their villages, but the families remained in the village only a few months at a time. During hunting season, they moved to hunting grounds, gathering seasonal plants as they moved. They named the animals and plants that they found around them and began to create rituals to explain the all-powerful deity, Wah'Kon-Tah. Because they spent most of the year in migration between forests and prairies, the Osage avoided some of the waves of European diseases that swept through other tribes.

The social organization of Sacred Sun's people was complex. It is unclear whether women enjoyed power and status equal to the men because records of the Osage do not predate the influence of European traders and settlers, whose

Osage families lived in well-furnished longhouses in their villages, but they were nomadic and for many months of the year were away on hunts. After planting a garden in April, the month of Planting Moon, the families walked to bison hunting grounds in the west. They spent June (Buffalo-Pawing Moon) and July (Buffalo-Breeding Moon) on the prairie, returning in August (or Yellow-Flower Moon.)

At home in their village, the men continued to hunt through September (Deer-Hiding Moon or Peacemaker Moon), October (Deer-Breeding Moon), and November (Buck-Rattling-Horns Moon or Coon-Breeding Moon). The women preserved the fresh meat and skins for winter and tended to clothing. Winter was the hardest season, when the major task was staying warm and well fed. January was Frost-on-Inside-of-Lodge Moon, February was The-Light-of-Day-Returns Moon, and March was the Just-Doing-That Moon, a month when food stores might be lowest, but there was hope that spring would soon appear. *Missouri Department of Natural Resources* presence transformed gender roles. Indeed, the Europeans who described the lives of the Osage assumed that the men were making the decisions. However, we know that each clan, made up of several extended families, had female leaders as well as male, and it appears that every member was valued for serving a special purpose.

In some tribes, Native American women had power over war and peace. The Oklahoma historian Carolyn Foreman and others have found many examples among Native American tribes of women intervening to persuade their men from killing; Foreman says that Shawnee female chiefs were appointed for war as well as peace. A peace chief would approach the war chief "and setting before him the care and anxiety and pain which the woman experienced in their birth and education she appeals to his better feelings and implores him to spare the innocent and unoffending against whom his hand is raised."

In 1788, a representative of the Iroquois had tried to explain the importance of Native American women to the governor of New York: "Our ancestors considered it a great offence to reject the counsels of their women. . . . They were esteemed as mistresses of the soil as they attend to the labours of agriculture. Who, said they, bring us into being? Who cultivates our land, kindles our fires, or administers food to the calls of the hungry, but our women?" Indeed, the historian Willard Rollings estimated that with corn, squash, pumpkins, and beans, Osage women's gardens provided as much as three-fourths of the diet for their families. Corn was so important that Osage ceremonies used corn as a symbol of life itself. A woman owned the produce she raised, and a surplus meant that she could trade for other things she wanted. This power to feed her family likely gave Osage women power in the political arena as well.

In the time of Sacred Sun's grandparents and parents, the Osage had benefited from trade but continued to practice their traditions. For example, according to Osage historian John Joseph Mathews, girls of that time grew up under the watchful eyes of "old duennas," or "whippers," who carried knives and threatened young men who might try to spy on them. Mathews says that "the Whippers . . . protected their girls for the strongest and bravest and handsomest warrior."

After Sacred Sun's birth, her mother would have strapped her firmly to a cradleboard cushioned with absorbent moss. The cradleboard could be fastened to a tree branch or to a post in the home and decorated with feathers and beads to amuse the infant as her eyes began to focus. From this vantage point, Sacred Sun could watch her mother work with the other women as they tended gardens, processed and preserved food, and made clothes and cooking implements.

It is interesting to reflect upon the account of a white woman who was captured by the Seneca, lived with the tribe for sixty-five years, and had five children with an Indian husband. She seemed to have enjoyed her life with the women of the tribe, who treated her as if she had "been born of their mother." She described her daily routine as "probably not harder than that of white women . . . we planted, tended, and harvested our corn, and generally had all our children with us, but had no master to oversee or drive us, so that we could work as leisurely as we pleased." When the woman, Mary Jemison, told her story at age eighty, she recalled that the cares of the Native American women were "not half as numerous, not as great" as those of white women.

Like other tribes, the Osage practiced religious rituals some-times puzzling to whites. Three times a day, they stopped to pray and give thanks. Osage historian John Joseph Mathews, the great-great-grandson of an early settler and an Osage woman, described what he called a "wailing prayer" as "a long, drawn-out chant broken by weeping. . . . It was like the song of the wolf . . . and it broke, too . . . with a soul-stirring sob."

Mathews observed that the prayer "always ended before it was finished, in a sob of frustration. It was Neolithic man talk-ing to God." Sacred Sun would awake each morning to these loud prayers of the villagers standing at the doorways of their longhouses.

Indian Girl with
papoose — fording
a Stream

The Burden Strap, by Alfred Jacob Miller. This young woman balances a cradleboard and baby safely on her back by using a burden strap. A young groom would honor his bride with the gift of a symbolic burden strap, a symbol of her virtues and prerogatives, carefully made for her with his own hands. *Joslyn Art Museum, Omaha, Nebraska*

Ceremonies and rituals helped mark the passage of time and were a way to celebrate the hard work of each season. Osage women sang special songs as they planted, to draw the protection of Wah'Kon-Tah, the great life spirit, to the gardens. A visitor described the dances of the young women, saying that they "execute the most extravagant dances, making them into incredible feats; they decorate their heads, their arms, and their legs with feathers, with porcupine quills, and with sinews of elk."

For Native Americans, everyday life was deeply connected to belief in higher powers, especially the power of the life force, Wah'Kon-Tah, who had divided the universe into air, earth, and water. According to their tradition, the Osage—who called themselves "ni-U-Ko'n-Ska," or "Children of the Middle Waters"—came to earth at Marais des Cygnes after Wah'Kon-Tah created it. One clan, Tzi-sho, the Sky People, descended from among the stars. They were the people of peace. On earth, they met the Hunkah, or Earth people, who held the secrets of war.

While the roles of each sex were different, the importance of each child was evident even to visitors. Washington Irving describes how an Osage father mourned the death of his young daughter. The distraught father killed his child's favorite pony and buried it with her so that she could ride it to the spirit world.

An Osage daughter like Sacred Sun began to learn women's work through imitating her mother and the other women. Her first steps would have brought great excitement to her young mother, because as soon as the baby walked, it was time for the formal naming ceremony. The naming ceremony marked the baby's passage into personhood, and a mother was serious and thoughtful as she selected her child's name. The child could earn other names as it grew, but a mother believed that her choice could shape her child's future—whether the child would be bold or shy, and whether it would attract good fortune or pity from Wah'Kon-Tah.

Osage children still play with dolls and cradleboards made like the toys used in the days of Sacred Sun. *Osage Tribal Museum, Pawhuska, Oklahoma; photo by A. E. Schroeder*

Both parents attended the ceremony, which was conducted by the most important Osage spiritual leaders, the "Little Old Men." For the naming ceremony, a mother decorated a buffalo robe with elaborate painted symbols of Grandfather the Sun, sewing the images of important creatures and plants in patterns made from flattened porcupine quills. The spring after the naming ceremony, the mother would plant seven hills of corn, and when it matured she would prepare a feast to serve to all those important in her child's future life. Alice C. Fletcher suggested in 1900 that Sacred Sun's name in the Osage language, Mohongo, or Mi-Ho'n-Gah, was similar to the Omaha "Mihunga," which means "woman leader, or chief."

Sacred Sun's people solved their most tricky problems by undertaking a quest and waiting for a sign from nature. The quests took days and usually succeeded only after several failed attempts. Often, the questioner fasted, finding answers in the appearance of unusual animals. All animals were venerated by the Osage as fellow travelers on the planet. Stories of the quests were retold, becoming oral traditions, passed on in ceremony and storytelling.

One important account illustrates the danger and imbalance that resulted when the relationship between groups in the tribe was overlooked, showing that only ritual and quest could correct such imbalance. Indeed, women contributed to the success of the quest. In this story from informants Mathews interviewed, a group of Osage scouts—the young men of the tribe—was crossing the prairie, carrying a sacred bundle of hawk skin, covered by a buffalo-hair weaving and deerskin. The scouts believed that the bundle had mystical qualities to protect them, but as they approached their village, a "blue-black cloud rose out of the northwest and . . . shot forth a crooked lance of lightning, killing several of the party." The bundle had not protected the hunters, so the elders would have to go on a quest to learn why it had failed and correct its vulnerability.

The elders went to their special place—the Lodge of Mystery—to think about how to improve the bundle. Days may have passed, but finally they realized that one part of the tribe—the Water People—had no symbol in the bundle. They decided that this was the bundle's weakness and sent young men out to find a water rush to be woven into a covering. The messengers went all directions.

One by one, the Little Old Men rejected the rushes the messengers brought. One young man, focusing on a half-moon lake, brought a rush from the border, then a "ribbed reed," then a large rush. Finally, he took off his moccasins and clothing and waded to the center of the lake, where he selected a thin rush. The Little Old Men "accepted this perfect rush immediately." The young man was "so proud that he only stood and looked into the distance menacingly, to veil his emotion, as the holy men praised him."

Now they needed a skilled woman to weave the rushes into a useful cloth. They taught her a song, which they had made for her—"a wailing song about death and the loved ones who had gone away." Because her work was sacred and private, she went to a small lodge next to her family lodge and slept. In the morning, she walked outside, put moist earth on her forehead, and, sitting on the ground with her legs straight out in front of her and close together, in the way Osage women sat, she began her task. She wove and sang for four days, sometimes remembering loved ones and breaking into wails of grief. On the fourth day, she displayed her weaving, which was approved by the Little Old Men.

They made the weaving into a covering, and the bundle from then on belonged to all Osage, although it was sacred and could not "be touched by anyone who has not the proper authority." The bundle now possessed the power of all Osage families, as well as the powers of both male and female. It satisfied the quest.

That a woman would play such an integral role in the quest for creating a protective bundle for hunters—a matter of life and death, as the Osage saw it—shows how women were valued for their own roles as nurturers and protectors of the tribe itself. Native Americans were totally dependent on the earth for their essentials as well as their luxuries, using dishes made from wood or clay, spoons from buffalo horn or shell, and kettles made from the paunch of the buffalo. It was the women who usually created these items, continually connecting the tribe to nature's gifts.

To be sure, the women were also the protectors and ultimate teachers of the tribal history. As one observer wrote, "the memory of the squaws is the principal repository of their historical treasures, for such are their traditions esteemed."

During the time of Sacred Sun's childhood, old songs, dances, traditions, and stories were still very important, but trading patterns were changing, and trade items had an impact on traditions. For instance, the Osage had long bartered with other tribes for useful things like stone and shells from other regions, but now European and American metal items had become so important to the Osage that the Little Old Men devised a ceremony to honor metal.

The Osage harvested furs from fox, beaver, wolf, bear, badger, and muskrat to trade for European tools and clothing. Osage hunting grounds, in the present states of Missouri, Kansas, Oklahoma, and Arkansas, were rich with deer, elk, and bison. In exchange for the furs, Sacred Sun's people obtained rifles and ammunition. Even though early rifles were inaccurate and hard to use, the Osage wanted to keep the weapons out of the hands of the western tribes. Additionally, even though the Osage stalked their prey on foot, they owned horses as early as 1682. There was a powerful psychological advantage to riding into battle with the sun glinting off rifle barrels, even though it was nearly impossible to fire a rifle from a horse and hit a moving target.

Almost a century before Sacred Sun was born, on a 1724 trip from Fort Orleans on the Missouri River to meet the western tribes, Etienne de Bourgmont had brought to the Indians guns, swords, hatchets, powder, bullets, woven cloth of red and blue, scissors, combs, shirts, needles, pots, bells, beads, wire, and a variety of ornaments. As Mathews observes, "It was similar to a modern television sponsor's giving away a car or a trip to Bermuda."

As imported fabric became available, women began to use it rather than animal skins to make wraparound skirts. It was not long before European fabric, beads, and metal pots replaced many of women's traditional products. Woven blankets from industrial woolen mills began to replace buffalo-skin robes; woven ribbons and glass beads replaced elk teeth, shells, and porcupine quills for decoration.

At the same time, women's leather-making skills gained economic value, because animal skins could not be shipped without preservation. Mathews wrote that the women brought pelts to the trading posts and left with beads, hawk bells, and mirrors. The shift in the economy changed women's lives. As William E. Foley put it, "The emphasis on hunting even altered marriage practices as Osage men began taking additional wives to handle the extra chores of cleaning and preparing the animal hides and skins."

Much of the power of women in the Osage and other tribes had come from their importance as agriculturalists, potters, food preparers, leather workers, and keepers of important trade secrets from generation to generation. As Europeans brought wool blankets to replace buffalo hides, and as glass beads began to replace decorations made from animal teeth, sea-shells, and porcupine quills, the perceived importance of the women, who had formerly harvested these goods for the tribe, was diminished.

During French colonial times, some French traders developed deep connections with Native American families, and many Osage women became guides, concubines, or wives of Frenchmen. In 1764, Pierre de Laclède and his stepson Auguste Chouteau founded St. Louis, and developed a fur trading post. The Osage enjoyed a long-standing connection with Laclède, Auguste Chouteau, his halfbrother Pierre, and their sons. The Chouteaus and their traders brought manufactured goods from Europe and the eastern United States to exchange for furs. Tanis Thorne, the author of *The Many Hands of My Relations,* reported that by 1777, 60 percent of the furs passing through St. Louis came from Osage traders. That percentage stayed relatively steady at 50 to 55 percent until after 1804, according to Thorne.

As Sacred Sun was growing up, American settlers moved into the Osage territory, replacing the French traders who had been there for more than a hundred years. In 1803, a few years before she was born, the United States purchased the land west of the Mississippi that had been claimed by the French. After the Louisiana Purchase, President Thomas Jefferson planned to move the southeastern tribes—including the Cherokee, Seminole, Creek, Choctaw, and Chickasaw—west of the Mississippi in order to make their ancestral lands available for American settlers in the east.

The Trapper's Bride. Artist Alfred Jacob Miller reported in 1850 that native girls were being sold to trappers, noting that the purchase price for this sale was six hundred dollars. The folklorist Rayna Green says, "For some traders, an alliance with an Indian woman ensured that they would always have food and shelter." A child from the union ensured that the man had a place in Native American society; the children often spoke both languages and moved between the two cultures. *Joslyn Art Museum, Omaha, Nebraska*

Jefferson thought the Osage and other western tribes could be convinced to clear the wilderness and establish farms, replacing their traditional nomadic hunting life with life in American-style villages. Some members of the five tribes in the southeast, known as the "civilized tribes," were already living peacefully on small acreages, keeping livestock, raising grain, and using slaves as labor.

Jefferson and others failed to take into account the hunting cultures of the western tribes or their close ties to the French. Dennis McAuliffe Jr., a journalist and Osage historian who wrote *The Deaths of Sybil Bolton: An American History,* notes that when the Osage learned that the Americans had purchased the territory, "they burned the letter. They didn't think much of Americans."

On May 14, 1804, after many months of preparation, Meriwether Lewis, the private secretary to Thomas Jefferson, and William Clark, a military leader, left St. Charles to explore the new territory, and Jefferson invited a delegation of Osage chiefs including the leader Pawhuska, called Chief White Hair, to Washington, D.C. The visit was intended to impress the Osage leaders with the wealth and power of the Americans, and to introduce the Osage to their new "father," Thomas Jefferson.

In 1806, the Lewis and Clark expedition returned to St. Louis from their "Voyage of Discovery." They had followed the Missouri River to its source and then traveled across land and by waterway to the Pacific Ocean and back. Their report of friendly Native Americans and plentiful land and resources seemed an invitation to explorers and settlers. Lewis wrote, "I think two villages on the Osage River might be prevailed on to remove to the Arkansas, and the Kansas, higher up the Missouri."

The Chouteaus took a group of Osage leaders—twelve chieftains and four boys—to Washington to meet the president and to secure the rights of trade in 1806. That year, northern Osage shipped $43,000 worth of furs through St. Louis, and southern Osage shipped $20,000 through Arkansas. With the new American government in place, the Chouteaus lost the monopoly on fur trade, but with their few competitors they kept fur prices low. Bearskins brought about $1.50 to $2.00 each, and small animal skins like fox and beaver 25 cents.

In 1808, William Clark, acting for the American government, presented the first of many treaties to the Osage leaders. The Americans asked for all Osage land south of the Missouri River and east of a line drawn from the site of Fort Osage, in present-day Jackson County, to the Arkansas River—about fifty thousand square miles. In return, they promised the protection of the U.S. government if the Osage moved to a village near Fort Osage, also called Fort Point, as Clark had written on his map, or Fire-Prairie Fort, or Fort Clark. This was the first American fort west of the Mississippi. The government promised to supply the Osage with a blacksmith, grain mill, plows, two log houses for their leaders, and a trading post. And, at the fort, the Osage would receive an annual payment or "annuity" of fifteen hundred dollars as long as they were peaceful.

Pierre Chouteau, who in 1807 regained from the territorial government an exclusive license to buy furs from the Osage, signed the 1808 treaty as agent for the Osage. Meriwether Lewis, by this time the governor of the Louisiana Territory, signed on behalf of the Americans. By this treaty, the Osage formally gave up much of their land, but most did not understand the importance of the treaty or recognize it as valid. In their tradition, individuals did not own land; instead, they used it in common.

George Sibley was the factor—or director—at Fort Osage. The fort stocked a variety of trade goods—blankets, cloth, traps, guns, ammunition, metal hatchets, knives, kettles, bells, and vermilion, a bright red dye, which soon replaced the natural red berries and earth used as face paint. Owned by the American government, the fort soon affected the business of the Chouteaus.

Though the Osage gave up their lands east of their Osage River villages in the 1808 treaty with the United States government and had agreed to remain near Fort Osage along the Missouri River, they continued to use their traditional hunting grounds, which included much of present-day Missouri, Arkansas, and Kansas. They were the first tribe to be met by American pioneers crossing the Mississippi River—and Americans were pouring into the territory. In 1800, there were an estimated 7,000; by 1804, 10,000. The number doubled to 20,000 by 1810.

As many as 5,000 Osage moved near the fort, but they continued to migrate away to hunt or moved back to the old village. They continued to observe their traditions as they always had, with morning prayers and ceremonial dances. Few Americans understood the Osage ceremonies. Henry Brackenridge, visiting Fort Osage in 1811, wrote that he had heard "the most hideous howling." He thought that it might be "partly devotional and if it be true as supposed by some that they offer worship only to the evil spirit . . . certainly [it was] not unworthy of him."

Brackenridge also reported seeing Osage men dancing over the scalps of seven Iowa. One of the dancers defiantly approached the fort and was captured and whipped by the soldiers. He returned to camp in disgrace, but other Osage joined him and marched angrily to the fort. Brackenridge wrote that the Osage had one admirable trait: "They are rarely if ever known to spill the blood of the white man." As Osage historian Mathews observed, this was not the case, as American pioneers in the Boonslick discovered.

Cherokees were flooding into Osage territory in Arkansas and American emigrants from the east were moving as far west as present-day Saline and Howard Counties in Missouri. The Americans brought their families, slaves, and livestock. According to Mathews, the Osage hated the new settlers' hogs, which smelled bad and destroyed the woods. Continual skirmishes and battles were becoming a way of life between

Native Americans and the new arrivals, especially during the War of 1812, when tribes friendly to the British raided American settlements.

Because they were afraid they could not protect it, the American government had ordered Fort Osage closed in the spring of 1813, much to the disappointment of George Sibley. He set up a trading house at Arrow Rock for a time, but the law permitting government trading houses expired in 1814. When a second law passed in 1815, Sibley was ready to return to Fort Osage with his fifteen-year-old bride, Mary Easton, daughter of the first postmaster of St. Louis. Her wedding trip was by keelboat up the Missouri River with her books, her piano, a large wardrobe, and her saddle horse.

Sacred Sun would have been about six years old when Fort Osage reopened and may have been among the Osage children who heard Mary Sibley play her famous piano with its fife and drum attachment. According to Sibley, the Osage "literally idolized" Mary after they heard her play the piano. She would have been among the first American women Sacred Sun would have known. When her younger sister visited her from St. Louis, Mary included young Osage in the lessons she gave her sister.

Soon after the Louisiana Purchase, alcohol had begun to make its way upriver with fur traders and whiskey peddlers. Although banned as a trade item by law in 1802, alcohol was often used in negotiating with Native Americans, and it was not illegal on lands set aside for half-blood descendants of early St. Louis merchants and traders. In spite of precautions, liquor had found its way to the Osage. Soon, Osage elders, who had traditionally been in control of the rituals of life, found their power undermined by factions who followed Chouteau's French-Indian descendants.

For generations, the Osage had left their villages almost unguarded while the men went on their summer and autumn hunts. In 1817, while many southern Osage men were away from their village, five hundred Cherokee and other eastern

Indians raided their village, destroying the storehouses and killing and wounding many Osage, mostly women and children. They took more than a hundred captives, sending some as slaves to Cherokees still in the east.

Willard Rollings writes that after this attack, "the Osage were ordered to go to St. Louis and surrender land to the Cherokee." At the meeting, Pierre Chouteau acted as agent for the Osage, with Paul Loise serving as translator. Rollings identifies Loise as "either Auguste or Pierre Chouteau's Osage son." The tribe was now completely split, with villages in two locations. One group lived at their traditional home on the Osage River while the other had moved to Arkansas. They would probably not have agreed to the 1818 treaty if they had understood it. They also would not have agreed with the American plan to take over the trade and replace the French with American-sanctioned traders.

Sacred Sun would have been about nine or ten years old at this time, growing up in a family allied with the Chouteaus. The Chouteaus wanted to reunite the tribes and bring their trade back to St. Louis, so they insisted that the 1818 treaty be written to move the distribution of the annuity from Fort Osage to St. Louis. Rollings believes that some of the Osage, living around St. Louis and trading with the French, "may have wanted all those things."

At the same time, the United Foreign Mission Society of New York established missions for each of the groups. Union at Fort Gibson, Indian Territory, was established for the southern Osage in 1820, and in 1821 Harmony Mission was built near the village on the Osage River. Both missions took Osage children from their families to educate them in Christian traditions. A teacher at Harmony Mission wrote in his diary that he found the Osage children "as interesting and active as the generality of children among the whites, and I have sometimes thought them more so."

The disruption of tribal life was especially hard for the women and young girls like Sacred Sun. In contrast to the

French, who came in small numbers and respected the Osage nomadic lifestyle, the new pioneers came by the hundreds to claim land, clear it, build fences, and establish farms. Whites were claiming the familiar Osage places, including the sacred resting places of loved ones who had died. As wild places became farms and villages, the native plants that Osage used for food and medicine began to disappear.

Big Soldier, a leader of the Little Osage, was well known for speaking out against the American way of life. Called l'Orateur, or "the speechmaker," by the French, his eloquent speech to the Americans was reported by George Sibley in 1820.

> I see and admire your manner of living, your good warm houses, your extensive fields of corn, your gardens, your cows, oxen, workhorses, wagons, and a thousand machines, that I know not the use of. I see that you are able to clothe yourself, even from weeds and grass. In short, you can do almost what you choose. You whites possess the power of subduing almost every animal to your use. You are surrounded by slaves. Everything about you is in chains, and you are slaves yourselves. I hear I should exchange my presents for yours. I too should become a slave. Talk to my sons, perhaps they may be persuaded to adopt your fashions, or at least to recommend them to their sons; but for myself, I was born free, was raised free, and wish to die free.

By 1821, the American population in the Missouri Territory had risen to over sixty-seven thousand—more than triple the number of 1810. By the end of the decade, enough white Americans lived in the territory that the residents could petition for statehood. Steamboats were traveling the Mississippi River and had ventured up the Missouri. Several river towns were growing into prosperous American centers where pioneers could buy the supplies they needed to go farther west. The Osage called the Americans "Long Knives" and, later, "Heavy Eyebrows," which was their old name for the French;

no matter what they were called, the increasing numbers of American emigrants disrupted Osage life even more.

The government continued to encourage the Cherokees to move from their homelands to Osage territory. After the 1817 attack on their village, the Osage had taken old men, women, and children on their hunts, but in 1821 some Cherokees raided a hunting camp, killing a dozen guards and twenty-nine women and children and capturing ninety. A missionary journal reported that at least three of the captives—a woman, her child, and a young girl—were "most barbarously murdered . . . and [they] threw their bodies to be devoured by the hogs."

The massacre interrupted the hunt, so the villagers were unable to feed themselves in the winter of 1821. They sought help in the other Osage villages. Soon all the supplies were gone and the entire nation faced starvation. One missionary wrote, "How distressed their situation at present. They have returned with no provisions and are very poor. Their situation called for our prayers and for the prayers of all good people."

Mathews reported that in the winter of 1821, all the Osage women mourned with wails that became sharp keening that could be heard for a long distance. To the Osage, the deaths by the Cherokee were particularly distressing because there was no chance to properly mourn the loss of their loved ones. The dead "would be compelled to wander restlessly over the earth as lost souls, unrecognized by Wah'Kon-Tah because their faces had not been painted" in the traditional manner.

Sacred Sun, now twelve or thirteen years old, was surrounded by war and starvation. The elders' stories about the old days must have seemed like fantasies. In traditional times, Sacred Sun would have married soon after puberty in a solemn ceremony that joined the two families as well as the young couple. Traditional courtship began when a young man completed his hunter's initiation. At that time, his uncle was charged with finding him a wise young woman from an unrelated Osage clan. The uncle would approach the young woman's family and call for her mother's brother. The two uncles would meet, each seeking approval from the family before going to the next stage. Days of ceremonial meetings and gift exchanges followed, each ceremony bringing in more family members. The negotiations ended with a feast.

The bride and groom were kept away from one another. Most likely, they had never seen each other. In her home, the bride was bathed and powdered "with a dark powder that came from a bean-like plant with leaves like an iris and an orchid-like flower, the powder coming from the seed pods." The groom remained in his parents' home, singing the Crow Song or the Wolf Song to himself. The relatives, getting to know each other, "wore smiles and bright faces."

On the fourth day, the bride came from her lodge and, with her bridesmaids, watched over a footrace, with prizes for the best runners, who were sometimes male and sometimes female. The families exchanged more gifts, and, finally, the groom was brought to sit next to his bride. The two presided over a feast, but they did not look at one another.

After the feast, the young man went to a private lodge and his attendants carried the bride to him. Now the young couple gazed at each other for the first time and spent the night together.

This ancient tradition was breaking down as Sacred Sun entered adulthood, and conflicting reports make it impossible to know exactly who and when she married. Mathews says that Sacred Sun was "possibly" married to Washinka Sabe, also called Black Bird, a "second chief," but a French publicity brochure of the time, "Six Indiens Rouges," says Sacred Sun was married to Little Chief, an important chief by birth and descendant of an Osage chief who had gone to France one hundred years earlier with Etienne de Bourgmont.

While she may have had an Osage husband, Sacred Sun apparently became the "country wife" of one of the Chouteaus or their close associates and became the mother of a mixed-blood daughter. The mother and child are mentioned in a treaty signed on December 30, 1825, and accepted by sixty

D'après nature par Mr Colson.   *Lith. de Langlumé rue de l'Abbaye, N°4*

In this portrait of the six Osage travelers by a "Mr. Colson," the Osage men wear native-style clothing and the women wear simple slippers and pleated dresses, a style that may have been set in 1806 when Pierre Chouteau took six Osage leaders and their wives to Washington. To present the women to the public without creating a sensation over their "immodest" dress, the wife of Secretary of War Henry Dearborn rejected suggestions that they should simply wear blankets over their native costumes or be dressed in silks and satins. She dressed them in plain, short dresses with petticoats made of bright, printed chintz. *State Historical Society of Missouri, Columbia*

Osage leaders including Big Soldier. This treaty moved the Osage completely out of the state of Missouri and the Territory of Arkansas, but several tracts of 640 acres on the north side of the Marais des Cygnes were set aside for French-Osage children, including one for "Amelia, the daughter of Mi-hunga"—evidence that "Mi-hunga," or Sacred Sun, had a child by one of the traders.

It was common for some prominent Frenchmen to have two families—one white family in St. Louis, which ensured membership in the elite society of the city, and an Osage or half-Osage wife in a separate village. Many Osage girls lived in the "country compounds" and may have been sold by their parents to the traders. After the starvation of the winter of 1821, this may have been the only choice for some parents.

Auguste Pierre Chouteau, nephew of Auguste, settled near Fort Gibson near present-day Muskogee, Oklahoma, and soon Chief Pawhuska and the Osage moved nearby. With a new license to trade with the Osage and Kickapoo, A. P. Chouteau was in charge of four Osage trading posts by 1825.

In return for the land gained in the treaty that moved the Osage out of Missouri, the United States was to pay off all Osage debts and make annual seven-thousand-dollar payments to the tribe; to furnish farming tools, teachers, and a blacksmith so the Osage could begin farming; and to provide 600 cattle, 600 hogs, 1,000 fowls, 10 yoke of oxen, and 6 carts.

A few months later, on May 3, 1826, the Osage ceded an indefinite amount of land to Americans for a road through the "half-breed" tracts. This incursion may have been the last straw to Big Soldier, Sacred Sun, and the four other Osage.

In 1827, these four men and two women of the Osage tribe traveled from their Missouri homeland to France. According to John Joseph Mathews, there was Ki-He-Kah Shinkah, or Little Chief, who was thirty-six. Then there was Mi-Ho'n-Ga, or Sacred Sun, who was eighteen. Washinka Sabe, or Black Bird, according to Mathews, was "possibly husband of Sacred Sun." Another young woman, named Gthe-Do'n-Wi'n, or

Hawk Woman, was nineteen. Mo'n-Sho'n A-ki-Da Tonkah, or Great Protector of the Land, was eldest at forty-five and "apparently called himself Big Soldier and was called by the French 'l'Orateur.'" Minckchatahooh, a twenty-two-year-old warrior, completed the group.

For Sacred Sun, especially, leaving on a long journey would have been difficult. She would have left her child, Amelia, behind. But the increasing number of American settlers had made life miserable for the Osage, and the travelers saw the French as their friends. Big Soldier, aligned with the French all of his life, was experienced in travel and, as the oldest of the group, would have seemed a leader to the others. To these travelers, the voyage may have fulfilled the dream of making a quest for signs and answers that would help the tribe. Or it may simply have been a chance for adventure.

Traveling with the Osage were David Delaunay, who organized the trip and acted as their guide, François Tesson, a St. Louisan from a French family, and Paul Loise. Delaunay, born in France, had been in the territory since 1800 and had been a close associate of Auguste Chouteau.

A century earlier, chiefs from the Missouri, Osage, Oto, and Illinois tribes had visited Paris, accompanied by a young woman from the Missouri tribe. Since that time, tales of the American west had kept Europeans keenly interested in Native Americans. Thus newspaper writers in France and the United States followed the story of the six Osage visitors. Thousands of Europeans saw them, and promoters described their tribal customs in at least two publicity brochures published in France.

Although newspapers in the U.S. and abroad followed the departure of the group and their arrival in France, details of the events do not always agree. Still, we have records from three points of view—Osage, French, and American.

Osage historian John Joseph Mathews picks up the story of the travels after the signing of the treaty of 1825, saying that Loise had been ordered to stay away from the Osage but was persuaded by David Delaunay to return and find Osage who would go on the trip. He found twelve willing to take their harvest of four years' worth of furs to sell in New Orleans. Their raft was wrecked on the way, and six turned back.

Six continued and sailed across the ocean, arriving in Le Havre, France, on July 27, 1827. In Le Havre, huge crowds lined the streets to meet the travelers. Newspapers reported that crowds hung over the bridges and swarmed the docks. M. P. Vissier, a French writer, described the scene: "Their costume, their arms, the color of their reddish-copper skin, the beauty and regularity of their immobile features, everything about them was an object of surprise. Everyone pushed near them, to touch their hands, and to receive from them a gesture gracious and full of nobleness."

Vissier also gives us an estimate of their height—the men were about 5 feet 5 inches and the women about 5 feet tall. Earlier travelers had estimated the Osage to be taller—around 6 feet.

According to Carolyn Foreman, their arrival was widely anticipated because a priest, Father Matthew Anduze, had come before them. Anduze was a missionary who had served in the Osage country and had returned to France. Foreman quotes a French newspaper, reporting that one of the Osage had told Anduze, "take our names, smooth the way for us, and say to our great father . . . the little chief, the black spirit and the big soldier and others are going to France."

A military escort took the Osage travelers from the ship to their apartment. Crushing crowds appeared everywhere the Osage went. At an evening opera performance, all eyes of the audience turned to the Osage rather than to the performers on stage. In return, the Osage were gracious and patient. Mathews notes that at the opera, Little Chief, "who was called 'Prince of the Missouri,' spoke to the crowd, saying, 'My brothers, the good things done for us by the French people have entered through my eyes to my heart.'"

From Le Havre, they went to Rouen. The newspaper reported that "the two young women are very coquettish and occupy

In Rouen, an artist painted the six sitting together in a box at the opera. The men are bare-chested, with several rows of beads and large medallions around their necks. They wear silver armbands on their upper arms and wrists, and headbands securing a few feathers. Each man's head is shaved and has a topknot. The women wear identical striped dresses trimmed in lace, with big buttons up the front. Their hairstyles signify memberships in particular clans. *State Historical Society of Missouri, Columbia*

themselves continually with their attire . . . it was difficult to induce them to leave their toilette before going to the play."

After Rouen, the group went to Paris. A month after their arrival, a notice appeared in French newspapers saying that curious spectators would have to obtain tickets to see the Osage in theaters or in their apartments. A newspaper describes one of the women, who appeared on the hotel balcony. She had a "small stature" and a face "full of sweetness." The observer

The Osage took daily baths to wash away evil; women, after bathing, scented their bodies with mint, calamus root, and columbine seed. Then, each mother would part her daughter's hair in the middle and drew a red line with clay earth or berries in the part, symbolizing the daily path of Grandfather the Sun. *Excerpted from Carl H. Chapman and Eleanor F. Chapman,* Indians and Archaeology of Missouri, *revised edition (Columbia: University of Missouri Press, 1983)*

noted her black hair parted down the center with the red line down the parting, representing the dawn road of Grandfather the Sun. She wore strands of pearls and a red blanket. "She wore everything that had been given her."

The many presents given by French admirers made the Osage targets for robbery. At one time, they went to court after a hotel servant stole "thirteen pieces of silver and some kashmir from them."

Delaunay, not a very good businessman, was apparently in charge of expenses for the trip. One opportunity to make money came when the Osage agreed to take part in a "Fête Extraordinaire." They would dance the native dances of Missouri, and Little Chief would ascend in a balloon with a balloonist named Depuis. Newspapers reported that Little Chief uttered a "piercing . . . chant several times while in the air." Mathews explains that the chant was a prayer-song, "asking for the power to stay afloat."

Vendors sold Indian dolls, workbags embroidered with Indians, Indian figures made of spiced bread, and bronze figures of the group "which the students used as paperweights." According to Mathews,

> French males were fascinated by the Osage women, even though one, Mi-Ho'n-Ga, Sacred Sun, wife of Black Bird, was obviously "enceinte" [pregnant] and had begun to weep in her yearning for home where she might give birth to her baby in their own village. This weeping brought on the keening of Hawk Woman and distressed Delaunay, who was now for some incredible reason going into debt.

Delaunay took the Osage from one place to another, trying to raise money and avoid creditors. In Ghent, he sued a writer for libel because of an article accusing him of exploiting the Osage. The lawsuit drew a large crowd to see the Osage, according to Mathews. As Delaunay's troubles continued, the Osage women "wept and played cards and smoked the long black cigars, and the men were kept close to their quarters."

On February 10, 1828, about six months after the Osage arrived at Le Havre, two babies were born. Most historians believe that Sacred Sun gave birth to twin daughters, who were baptized in the church of St. Denis. Carolyn Foreman writes, "The daughters were well and strong, and one of them was of a much lighter complexion than her sister," suggesting that the babies' father was white.

Wealthy women of Brussels served as godmothers, and the babies received European names. Mathews says "Maria Theresa Ludovica Clementina Black Bird was adopted by a very wealthy woman of Liege and died the next year, while Maria Elizabeth Josepha Julia Carola remained with her mother."

Holding her baby daughter, Sacred Sun must have thought for a moment about the ancient Osage naming rites, the name received in a sacred shelter made of logs and animal skins. Osage mothers chose names that represented noble qualities from nature. In a traditional Osage naming, the Little Old Men would have told familiar stories and sung traditional songs.

But now they were in France. In the tradition of European Catholics, newborn infants received names from a list of saint names, in memory of the particular saint's qualities and holy days. The Catholic ceremony was conducted in Latin, a language few people knew, recited by a priest in a robe.

And there remains a hard question: Why did Sacred Sun give away one of her babies? Did the desperate Osage travelers sell it?

With one remaining infant, Sacred Sun must have worried about her daughter's future. It was winter, and the travelers were far from home. They began a long trek across Europe; they were reportedly in Amsterdam, Dresden, Frankfurt, and Berlin. Then, when the baby was almost a year old, on January 12, 1829, an article that appeared in Munich was widely reprinted in France:

> The Osages abandoned at Fribourg, Breslau, by their conductor have been brought here by a friend of humanity; they find themselves in the greatest destitution, suffering from hunger. When did these savages, welcomed in the courts, applauded at theaters, become the concern of the public? Today, curiosity no longer attracts the crowds; at least charity should sympathize with these unfortunates who are without friends; without a country, abandoned in a land they do not know, isolated by the language and their habits . . . in civilized Europe.

It took more than a year to collect enough money to send the Osage back to America. They had somehow split into two groups, and it is still unclear who was in each group. Mathews reports that Sacred Sun, her baby, Black Bird, and Minckcha-tahooh came to the attention of the Marquis de Lafayette, the French hero of the American Revolutionary War who had been to Missouri a few years earlier as a guest of the Chouteaus. He raised money to help the Osage get home, and he award-ed each with a medal carrying his image. They sailed from Bordeaux in April 1830.

Other sources suggest that Sacred Sun and her baby trav-eled home, with the help of Lafayette, but with Little Chief, Big Soldier, Paul Loise, and Loise's son who was age thirteen or fourteen. Because travelers later saw Big Soldier with a Lafayette medal, this version of the story sounds likely, but it is also possible that Lafayette presented medals to each of the six Osage.

Sacred Sun and the baby arrived alone in Washington, D.C.; Thomas McKenney, director of the Bureau of Indian Affairs from 1824 to 1830, wrote that Black Bird and Minckchatahooh died of smallpox while on the ship from France.

As soon as he learned that Sacred Sun and her baby were in Washington, McKenney arranged to have their portraits painted. He believed that the Indian way of life was doomed and that helping them adopt an American lifestyle was the only way to help them. As a record of their existence, he hired artists to paint portraits of every Native American who came to the nation's capital. The portraits were hung in a hall, and people paid to see them.

Thomas McKenney described the portrait of Sacred Sun, whom he called "Mohongo," as "lighted up with intelligence . . . joyous as well as reflective." He explains: "Escaped from servile labour, she had leisure to think. New objects were con-tinually placed before her eye; admiration and curiosity were often awakened in her mind; its latent faculties were excited. . . . If our theory be correct, the example before us affords a

Mohongo. After her return from France, the American artist Charles Bird King painted a famous portrait of Sacred Sun and her baby daughter. Thomas McKenney wrote a description to accompany the portrait: "Of the early life of this female we know nothing; and perhaps, little could be gathered that would be worthy of record. She is interesting on account of the dignity and beauty of her countenance, and the singular nature of her adventures since her marriage." *State Historical Society of Missouri, Columbia*

While Mathews says that Sacred Sun, Black Bird, and Minckchatahooh stayed together, this portrait of "Gretomih, Minckchetahooh, and Kishagashugah" by French artist L. Boilly suggests that these three were in one group while Sacred Sun, Black Bird, and Big Soldier were in the other. *State Historical Society of Missouri, Columbia*

significant and beautiful illustration of the beneficent effects of civilization upon the human mind."

The second group of travelers, including, perhaps, Little Chief, Hawk Woman, Big Soldier, and Paul Loise and his son, stayed several more months in France with Louis William Du Bourg, Bishop of Montauban, who had been in St. Louis from 1817 to 1826. As this group boarded their ship at Le Havre, Delaunay's creditors seized their luggage and gifts, including the Lafayette medals. These were later recovered and sent to them.

In Washington, Paul Loise was reunited with his wife and family. A letter to McKenney from a General Hughes says, "Of course he stays here with his family . . . his heart-broken child and squaw have gone to their nation and he is now here"—suggesting that Loise was perhaps the father of Sacred Sun's daughter.

The Osage travelers reached their new homes in the Oklahoma Territory near Fort Gibson in the summer of 1830. Louis Richard Cortambert wrote that he saw Sacred Sun and Little Chief in 1833 when Little Chief was presiding over a treaty conference at Fort Gibson. Little Chief must have been thinking about his adventures in France when he told the crowd: "I have traveled all over the world to learn the means to render my people happy, without success." In a treaty signed in 1839, Little Chief was awarded a house worth two hundred dollars.

Washington Irving reported that he saw Sacred Sun at the Chouteau country compound in 1835. In a letter to William Clark dated January 26, 1836, Thomas McKenney wrote that she had died of smallpox. According to the artist John Mix Stanley, he saw Big Soldier and painted his portrait at Tahlequah, Oklahoma, in 1843. Big Soldier, said Stanley, died in 1844.

For More Reading

For brief biographies on many of the Chouteau and Laclède families, plus a biography of Big Soldier, see Lawrence O. Christensen, William E. Foley, Gary R. Kremer, and Kenneth H. Winn, eds., *Dictionary of Missouri Biography* (Columbia: University of Missouri Press, 1999).

The Many Hands of My Relations: French and Indians on the Lower Missouri, by Tanis C. Thorne (Columbia: University of Missouri Press, 1996), explains the origins of the Osage-French mixed-blood, or "métis," society and culture in the eighteenth- and nineteenth-century fur trade.

The Osages: An Ethnohistorical Study of Hegemony on the Prairie-Plains, by Willard H. Rollings (Columbia: University of Missouri Press, 1992), examines the changes that took place in Osage society as a result of contact with the French, Spanish, and Americans.

The Osage in Missouri, by Kristie C. Wolferman (Columbia: University of Missouri Press, 1997), is a well-researched and readable account of Osage life in Missouri after the Louisiana Purchase.

The Osages: Children of the Middle Waters (Norman: University of Oklahoma Press, 1961) is by John Joseph Mathews, who based his writings on his own observations and interviews made in the 1920s with the old people he knew. Their stories, handed from generation to generation, went back two or three centuries to the time before European contact. The account of the trip to France is on pp. 539-47.

Emily Newell Blair

Hardly knowing what I did, I rose, pulled off my hat, and advanced to the front of the platform. What I would say I hadn't the slightest idea. . . . But words came tumbling out of the white heat which had somehow fused together all the things I felt unfair for women, all that I wanted for women, into an appeal for suffrage. Suddenly, to my surprise, it was a sign and symbol of what I wanted to fight for, it was a flag, a rallying point for women. At last I stopped, the torrent spent. And suddenly I was shaking as with a chill.

—From *A Woman of Courage,* by Emily Newell Blair, 1931

$\mathcal{E}$ mily Jane Newell was born in the Victorian era, when women's roles were limited to taking care of the home and family, teaching, or nursing. Over the course of her life, however, women gained more opportunities to pursue education and careers. Emily herself worked tirelessly for change and is most remembered for her role in the suffrage movement—helping win for women the right to vote.

Born on January 9, 1877, in Joplin, Missouri, she was the oldest daughter of James Patten Newell, a prominent businessman, and Anna Gray Newell, his wife. As a young man in Franklin, Pennsylvania, James had made a fortune, then lost it. He went west on the advice of Anna, and when they later met in Maysville, Kentucky, where Anna was visiting an aunt, they got married.

The Newells placed a high value on education for all their children. They insisted that Emily and her closest brother, Jim, be treated alike. Friends and neighbors nicknamed the two "Emily and Jimily." All her life, Emily was able to meet men on equal terms at a time when other women felt themselves separate from the male world.

In southwest Missouri, the period of industrialization after the Civil War was a time of many economic, cultural, and social changes. The city of Joplin had not existed before the war. In 1873, the town was founded by the Reverend Harris G. Joplin, who established the first Methodist church in Jasper County. Lead was discovered, the railroad came, and Joplin boomed, quickly growing larger than Carthage, the Jasper County seat. By 1900, Joplin's population was twenty-six thousand, making it the fourth-largest city in the state, a rough-and-tumble mining town where saloons lined the streets.

While the city drew families from surrounding farms, the most prominent people were connected with mining and the railroad. They came from industrialized areas and continued their strong ties with cities like Philadelphia, Chicago, and Cleveland. These newcomers built the industries, but they lived apart from the earlier settlers.

Anna Newell's father had served in the Union army during the Civil War, a source of family pride that also put the Newells in an uneasy position among their neighbors, many of whom had been harassed by Northern sympathizers in the Civil War. Virginia Jeans Laas, who edited *Bridging Two Eras,* Emily's autobiography, writes that the family "never overcame the feeling that they were eastern transplants, immigrants from afar."

Emily's father first worked in the mines and then became a bookkeeper, but he was elected Jasper County recorder in

1882. After his election, the family moved to Carthage, which was a more established and sedate community. In her autobiography, Emily remembered helping her father enter deeds into the county records when she was nine or ten years old.

After Emily and Jim, the Newells had four more daughters. As the oldest of six, Emily had responsibility for the younger ones, and she later wrote that she liked the feeling of community in a large family. Her parents encouraged her to think through problems and take charge when the need arose. These characteristics served her well in her schoolwork, but she remembered in her autobiography that she was not popular. Passing notes with a friend, Emily "rhapsodized over a poem of Robert Burns I had just read," but the other girls were not interested in poetry.

"I didn't know what to talk to them about. They thought me stiff and priggish, and probably I was, but this made it no easier," she wrote. "My defense was to shine at school." Being a good student did not increase her popularity, and to add to her youthful agony was a "martyrdom over . . . clothes." Instead of allowing her to wear the same fashions as the other girls, Emily's mother dressed her in hand-me-downs from a friend in Pennsylvania. "It was not economy that made Mother fix these dresses over for me so much as her belief that they were nicer than anything she could buy in Carthage," she wrote.

Emily remembered that her mother was not interested in housekeeping, and was "the last woman in the world to have had a large family." While her mother felt a strong sense of duty toward her children and took good care of them, her main interest was in being "a wife and student." On vacation days, her mother insisted that the children come to breakfast at eight and spend the mornings doing something constructive. Besides teaching the children to cook, her mother taught them French, a subject not available in the public school.

Many years after her mother died, Emily wrote that their mother had given each child a special gift: "my writing and interest in politics, Annie her leaning toward a religious life,

Julia her gift for music." Her mother's emphasis on education helped Emily prepare for a life of serious thought. In an unusual role for a young woman, she made a speech at her 1894 high school graduation. "Her points were cleverly given," the newspaper reported. The family agreed that Emily, unlike many other girls, would go to college.

She was encouraged to express herself independently, and she was also fortunate that there was money for her education. Her father had started a business making mortgage loans and was able to send Emily east to attend the Woman's College of Baltimore, now Goucher College. Arriving on the campus, however, she felt separate from the eastern women. "For the first time, I realized I was a westerner," she wrote, "a Missourian."

In June 1895, after Emily had attended college just one year, her father died, leaving her mother with children to raise and bills to pay. "My father died on Monday. He was buried on Saturday. And on Monday morning my mother went down to his office and took charge of his business," Emily wrote.

From the beginning, Emily's father had talked over business decisions with his wife, so with sixteen-year-old Jim, Emily's mother felt prepared to operate the three-hundred-thousand-dollar business. This was a highly unusual job for a woman at a time when most were completely dependent on husbands, fathers, or other male relatives.

Anna, however, felt she could not run both the business and the household, so at age eighteen, Emily returned home. A few years later, she found work as a teacher to help supplement the family income. A summer class at the University of Missouri in 1898 was her last bit of formal education.

On Christmas Eve of 1900, Emily married a high school classmate, Harry Wallace Blair, and changed her name to Emily Newell Blair. "The greatest stroke of luck I ever had was my husband," she wrote later. The wedding, at home, required decorating the entire house. Bedrooms were converted into elegant dining rooms, where one hundred guests sat down to a wedding supper.

Her mother had given her enough money to indulge herself in a new wardrobe, including "short skirts," which came four inches off the floor and were intended to be worn on outings with high-laced shoes, and dresses that swept the ground for afternoon parties and evening dances. Like the dresses, her numerous petticoats were handmade, and her stockings were silk. "It was the beginning of an extravagance that was to ride me all my days," she confessed.

The newlyweds returned east so Harry could attend law school in Washington, D.C. Their first child, Harriet, was born in Washington in 1903. Emily later wrote that her pregnancy surprised her mother, who commented, "No mother wants her daughter to be childless, but she never feels that the convenient season for her to have them has quite arrived."

The Blairs returned to Carthage where Harry began law practice. A year later, Jim helped them finance a house, which Emily remodeled. She insisted on having things exactly as she wanted them and was not intimidated by a contractor who said she must compromise. Before the project ended, she had antagonized all but two workers, who completed the job, and she had spent much more money than the original budget.

A son, Newell, was born in 1907. As a young wife with a son and a daughter, Emily was happy. The household also included hired servants to help with the large amount of work in keeping a house at a time when every household chore, from cooking to mending to cleaning to laundry, was done by hand. "I thought of myself," she wrote, "as the woman behind the scenes, the inspiration, the helpmate of them all."

Emily, like other middle- and upper-class women, was able to afford store-bought clothing and prepared food. She and her friends had servants who relieved the women of household work. The women gained leisure time, joined clubs, and read newspapers and magazines. There was plenty of volunteer work to do. They supported orphanages and promoted education for children.

While it was typical for well-to-do families to include servants, the employment boom made help expensive. In September 1909, the Blairs joined twenty other families in establishing a cooperative kitchen. They rented a large home, hired a manager, rented out the upstairs rooms, and then converted the first floor into a dining area. The kitchen stayed in business until January 1, 1912.

Emily later wrote that one day, while dining in the Cooperative Kitchen with a variety of other people, she realized that "women were to be entertaining, not argumentative. I tried to conform to this requirement." She had strong opinions, however, and one night she argued with two politicians that it seemed "as silly to elect your county recorders and treasurers and collectors as it would be to elect your butcher, baker, or banker; why didn't we elect one board, turn the county business over to it, and let it engage clerks to do the work?" As a woman, her opinion was irrelevant at the time because she would never have been able to vote for her plan, and her idea was dismissed as "infantile, impracticable, and silly." Later, however, she wrote an article about her idea of having a shorter ballot, and she mentioned in her autobiography that the article was "often referred to in college textbooks."

Emily kept trying to put her ideas into words. When the Blairs joined a discussion club, Emily took part fully and even argued for democracy against a man who was "a believer in aristocracy." He then "flattered me by saying I had a man's mind."

People all over the United States were thinking about the meaning of democracy. The year of Emily's marriage, 1900, is the date historians use to mark the beginning of the Progressive Era in American history. Until then, there were few laws requiring businesses to treat laborers fairly or to provide safe working conditions. Workers were expected to work long hours for little pay. Europe and the United States were rushing into industrialization, which would soon change the home from the busy, self-sufficient unit it had been for centuries. Rather than creating most of their necessities, like food and clothing, families were becoming dependent on manufactured goods. Factory-made clothing began to replace homemade, and large canneries did the work of food preservation. It took money to buy the factory-made items, so a new economy developed. Factory jobs away from home replaced women's work at home.

Industrialization brought a new standard of living, but there were problems as well as advantages. With no labor laws, people worked long hours in mines and factories. And with few quality controls in place, businessmen were free to take advantage of consumers by selling them spoiled food or shoddy products at high prices.

Child labor was a particular problem. Because large families needed all the money they could earn, parents began putting children to work rather than keeping them in school. By 1900, 76 percent of Missouri children ages six through twelve were in public schools, but the laws still allowed fourteen-, fifteen-, and sixteen-year-olds to work up to fifty-four hours per week, or six nine-hour days. Inspectors were supposed to make sure the laws were not broken, but parents, the youths themselves, and employers lied about children's ages to the point that even younger children were working long hours.

Children usually had the lowest-paid, most dangerous factory and mine jobs, often working in tight spaces too small for adults. Women leaders were among the strongest advocates for new laws to regulate child labor. Women also wanted laws to bring education, playgrounds, and recreational opportunities to children. They wanted to clean up city water supplies and the stifling air pollution caused by the factories. They also wanted laws to guarantee that manufacturers would produce better foods and protect working children and women.

Women had no power to vote for new laws, so they had to accomplish their political goals by joining with like-minded husbands and other men. Still, they made great strides. As a sign of their increasing political strength, by 1910, an American woman had the right to receive property from a will or to will property herself. Also, although a woman's earnings had once belonged to her husband, women could now keep the money they earned.

These rights helped women who were widowed, divorced, abandoned, or who wished to remain single, but few women understood the new laws. It was still customary for a woman to marry and stay in the marriage even if the husband treated her cruelly. Society still looked down on single women, but there were exceptional, independent women paving the way for the rest.

One exceptional single woman, Ella Harrison, born in Ohio, lived in Carthage from 1890 to 1900. She was a pioneer in her time, pursuing careers in teaching, farming, news reporting, and adventure. In Carthage, she devoted herself to women's suffrage, and others became interested because of her work. While there is no direct evidence that Harrison befriended young Emily, Harrison was well known in the region and had a wide influence.

Ella Harrison, in turn, had been influenced by a long line of women hopefully passing the desire for women's suffrage from generation to generation. As early as 1848, women asking for the right to vote had held a national meeting in Seneca Falls, New York, but just as the movement was gaining steam the Civil War turned attention to the slavery issue. When slavery was abolished, the Fifteenth Amendment to the Constitution guaranteed the vote for all men regardless of "race, color, or previous condition of servitude." Still, women could not vote.

All the same, women had learned that to win political battles they must work together and enlist the help of men. An international suffrage campaign was heating up in England and the United States. As early as 1867, ten St. Louis women met to form the Woman Suffrage Association of Missouri. In 1879, the National Woman Suffrage Convention met in St. Louis. Soon after, women in other Missouri communities founded their own suffrage societies. In 1910, ten prominent

Norborne, 1910. This parade for women's suffrage took place in Norborne, Missouri, in 1910. *State Historical Society of Missouri, Columbia*

St. Louis women came together and announced that the suffrage movement was "in full swing in the East and West . . . St.
Louis, occupying a central position, should put herself on
record as being in the ranks of our foremost cities."

The first suffrage lecture in Missouri was given by Miss Ethel
Arnold, a suffrage activist from England. She asked, "What are
municipal, state and national governments but housekeeping
on a large scale?" She continued, "Everyone knows that women
are naturally more economical than men." Suffragists all over
the state picked up the idea of women's natural abilities in
management.

The suffragists did not argue with the men who were in
charge. Instead, they pointed out that women were naturally
skilled in financial and community issues. Women managed
money. Women made budgets and paid for household help.
No one could argue with these points, and the women stayed
focused on their facts.

Also in 1910, Emily sold her first article to *Cosmopolitan*. She
wrote the article—"Letters from a Contented Wife"—just for
fun, but she sold it for the magnificent sum of $142.42. "I did
think that I had found a gold mine," she wrote later. Harry surprised her with a typewriter and an office desk delivered to the
house. She quickly produced and sold two other stories.

Then, financial tragedy struck: Her brother Jim's business
failed. Emily's mother, a sister, and Emily's family combined
resources in one small house. If Emily wanted to work on the
suffrage campaign, her wishes again became secondary to her
family's survival. She turned her attention more fully to her
writing, and soon her articles about homemaking and family
had appeared in *Cosmopolitan, Forum, Century, Ladies Home
Journal,* and other magazines. In 1913, she helped form the
Missouri Women's Press Association, and when the Missouri
suffragists started a magazine in 1914, they asked Emily Newell
Blair to be the editor. *The Missouri Woman* carried articles
about the law, women's rights, efficient household management, and the progress toward suffrage.

Besides her family obligations, Emily divided her time between writing and suffrage work. When suffragists forced a votes-for-women amendment into a statewide referendum in 1914, she plunged into the effort to get it passed. She was fortunate to have family support. So that Emily could work on suffrage, her mother took the children to visit a sister in Colorado. Some friends thought her family would be ruined because of Emily's new occupation, but her husband, Harry, supported her effort, even helping her mail press releases to inform newspapers about the cause.

The amendment failed, but Emily was rewarded with a trip to the national suffrage convention. The event was exhilarating and made the hard work worthwhile. "If I could just convey what it meant to this self-conscious, unimportant little woman from her small Missouri town," she wrote. At one dinner, she was seated next to Jane Addams, an internationally known suffragist and pacifist. Addams believed that problems should be solved in a nonviolent way, and she was dedicated to making life better for the poor. "I did feel, as I looked into those eyes, in which the sorrows of the world seemed to be mirrored, that here was a woman to reverence," Emily wrote. When she returned home, she devoted even more time to suffrage and *The Missouri Woman*.

The magazine reached a large number of readers because the Federation of Women's Clubs and the Parent-Teacher Clubs used *The Missouri Woman* to carry their news. Seeking to appeal to all kinds of women, the magazine also carried homemaking tips, poetry, and bits of humor. A column in May 1916 ran nursery rhymes for modern children:

> Jack and Jill
> Have equal will
> And equal strength and mind.
> But when it comes to equal rights
> Poor Jill trails far behind.

Another column ran this joke:

> "How long have they been married?"
> "About five years."
> "Did she make him a good wife?"
> "No; but she made him an awfully good husband."

Later that year, Blair offered a free year's subscription "to any woman sending in a recipe warranted to win a man to suffrage."

Blair kept divisive opinions out of the magazine and stayed away from controversial issues like prohibition, which she thought would divide suffrage supporters. Some articles were, however, particularly critical of the fashion industry. Successful housekeeping depended on thrift, and the articles encouraged women to economize and not to try to keep up with all the latest "fashion plates." The "suffrage style" was practical, dark-colored, and decorated simply.

In her own life, Blair tried to follow that advice, but she always confessed to a weakness for nice clothes. While she compared homemaking to business and wrote about how to buy carefully and save for purchases, her spending habits were always a problem. The family teased her that she was not able to follow her own advice to be thrifty.

By 1916, the suffrage cause had gathered momentum. The National Democratic Convention was to be held in St. Louis, and women from all over the state and nation were ready to demonstrate for a suffrage plank in the party platform. With their vision firmly fixed on getting the vote, the leaders wisely decided not to speak on issues that might divide them. Instead, they decided to build a coalition of women from all backgrounds—industrialists, laborers, housewives, Protestants, Catholics, Jews. How would they stand in agreement? They would remain silent. Emily remembered in her autobiography that she was the one who first suggested: "Why not . . . line the way to the Coliseum with women holding out their hands in mute appeal?"

The Missouri Woman, edited by Emily Newell Blair, was an important link between suffrage leaders and women at home. *State Historical Society of Missouri, Columbia*

The Democratic Convention was called to order and, while the men were meeting inside the convention hall, the women quietly assembled outside. In the style of the time, they were dressed in long, full skirts, and each carried a yellow parasol. Each woman also wore a yellow sash inscribed with the words "Votes for Women." "Nothing unladylike about a yellow sash," wrote Emily. The vigil lasted for six hours, "blocks and blocks of us, women from the tenements and some from New York mansions, teachers and housewives, factory workers and factory owners."

. The male delegates leaving the convention hall and walking down Locust Street found they were trapped in the silent, solemn "Golden Lane" for ten blocks. Some were "uncomfortable, some annoyed, and some nodding approval according to their opinions." A newspaper poet summed up the mortification of the delegates:

> Silence! My but it did talk . . .
> Fast the delegates did walk . . .
> But they couldn't get away
> From the Women's Votes display.
> They'll all recall for many a day
> Marching down the Golden Lane.

Despite opposition, the delegates were convinced that the time for woman suffrage had come, and grudgingly added "votes for women" to their platform for the presidential election.

Soon after this demonstration of voicelessness, the suffragists called a meeting in Atlantic City, New Jersey. In spite of many family obligations, Emily attended. Most of the leaders of the movement gathered at the convention, along with leaders from the Woman's Trade Union, Children's Bureau, House of Corrections, and other interest groups. President Woodrow Wilson addressed the group—the first time a president had paid attention to the issue of woman suffrage. As he spoke, he became "converted" to suffrage, and success for an amendment

The Golden Lane. When the male delegates came out of their meeting during the 1916 Democratic convention, they found the street lined on both sides by women standing silent. The action compelled men to put a suffrage plank in the Democratic party platform. *Western Historical Manuscript Collection–St. Louis*

seemed certain. Emily felt a rush of pride—she had helped bring this issue to the political front! At the same time, she felt guilty that she was, once again, away from home. Her roles of writer, suffragist, mother, and wife seemed overwhelming.

In her autobiography, she writes that she spent the week after the convention in a "small, cheap hotel." She lay on the beach alone and watched the water. "I spoke to no one. I did not even open a book. . . . At the end of the week I was a new woman."

Returning home, she felt she was regarded as a "sinner" because her family had needed her. Harry was under pressure after opening a new law firm. "Something had gone out of our relationship." The children had been left "too long" with friends. Once again, Emily felt that she must make a choice between home and work. Pulled from one role to the other, she resigned from her clubs, and in November 1916 gave up her job as editor of *The Missouri Woman*. "I settled down again to being a wife and mother."

Yet Emily knew that if she gave up her activism and writing careers completely, she might become "a dominant mother and nagging wife." Although the politicians had endorsed suffrage for women, World War I was raging in Europe, and it seemed evident that the United States would soon be involved.

War brought a great need for women's labor. They were needed at home, in industry, and as fund-raisers and volunteers. Women gathered supplies to send to soldiers and made bandages. Women had to fill factory jobs as men entered the military. In 1917, for the first time, the armed forces recruited women. The new working women also had to feed the family and care for children.

When the U.S. Council of National Defense set up a Woman's Committee, Blair was appointed a Missouri vice chairman. The committee issued bulletins about how to manage housekeeping and food during wartime. Child welfare, education, health, and recreation were familiar issues to the suffragists, and now they became a matter of patriotism and national survival. Emily threw herself into the new challenge even though she was "temperamentally a pacifist." Emily wrote, "I felt Jane Addams had hold of some mystical truth that I almost but did not quite grasp."

World War I scattered members of the Blair family. Harry was with the YMCA in France. Daughter Harriet was sent to boarding school. Emily went to Washington, D.C., in 1918 for several months to write for the Woman's Committee. She and Harry had been in Washington many times, and as early as 1902 she had wanted to live there. "Either one likes Washington or one does not," she wrote, "I was one who did. I would have been satisfied to stay."

Once again, she called on her mother for support, and Anna came to Washington and helped care for eleven-year-old Newell. Even though Emily was able to concentrate on work, she wrote in her autobiography: "I have always regarded those war months in Washington as a black, and very black, mark against my motherhood . . . not fair to Newell." Because she had been "overwhelmed mentally and repressed emotionally," she felt she had neglected the children. Newell, however, gained a measure of independence and pride. By taking care of himself while his father was in France and his mother was very busy, Newell felt he was helping win the war.

Summarizing the work of the Woman's Committee, Emily later wrote, "War work had opened up tremendous possibilities to women for public service . . . how can this energy and spirit be utilized for the country's benefit?" The answer was that women's work in World War I finally convinced politicians that women should have the vote.

In January 1918, suffrage gained a victory in Great Britain when the vote was granted to women who owned property. In the United States, several western states had gained suffrage. Then, on April 5, 1919, Missouri governor Fredrick D. Gardner signed a law to allow Missouri women to vote in the presidential election. A few months later, the U.S. Congress passed the Nineteenth Amendment, which declared that the right to vote "shall not be denied . . . on account of sex." The amendment was ratified on August 26, 1920.

Soon after the law was signed, Blair wrote the foreword for an issue about the suffrage movement for the *Missouri Historical Review*. Like most suffragists, Emily felt that women would vote as a bloc and thus elect candidates that had women's issues at heart. "Any change in the electorate of a democracy may affect the whole structure of its government. The elevation of almost half the population of a country from a position of political serfdom to that of equal authority . . . makes possible, at least, great changes." That dream did not become reality, however.

The Blairs returned to Missouri in 1919, and Emily threw her energies into her writing. "Social life of every kind was eliminated . . . even my housework came second. For the first and only time in my life I neglected it, but the neglect was deliberate. . . . I had to find out once and for all whether or not I could learn to write well enough to derive an income."

In her autobiography, Blair reports that she worked at writing steadily for nine months and produced "a million words of copy and read a great many books." She said this experience strengthened her faith in a "power, not ourselves, directing our circuitous ways," and helped her later advise women to prepare "to do the thing they feel 'led' to do."

Her work during the war, and the success of women's suffrage, liberated Emily. Her family now accepted and even expected her to work outside of her home, and her work became more focused. "I thought in terms of longtime programs on such things as child welfare, women in industry, high cost of living, prison reform."

After the rush of success, the reality of women's voting was disappointing. Emily was annoyed that women took their vote for granted and voted with their husbands, giving men "two votes instead of one in party matters." The suffragists had expected things to change quickly as women gained voting power. Certainly, the suffragists thought, with women voting, there would be an end to the abuses of the industrial system. Certainly, now, there would be free education for all, safe food laws, and equal opportunities for everyone.

Instead, voting brought new challenges. Many women let their husbands, fathers, or other men tell them what to do and how to vote. Now the challenge became to educate the new voters. Soon after the new suffrage law was signed, Blair helped create the League of Women Voters, an association that brought members of all political parties together for education and debates. She believed that informed women would become a force and gain the power that they wanted.

Through her work with the League of Women Voters, Blair

began to believe that women needed to act more boldly. At the same time, men thought that the league would become a threatening new "women's party" that would vote as a bloc and overthrow men. This controversy distracted voters from the issues that had interested Emily, so she left the league and put her energy into the Democratic party, which was also trying to bring women into the political process.

The Democratic leadership reasoned that a woman serving as vice chairman of the party would make women feel welcome, and they realized that they needed votes to stay in power. Charl Williams from Tennessee was the first Democratic national committeewoman and became a Democratic party vice chairman in 1921. The position, however, was honorary rather than functional.

The Missouri Democrats needed a committeewoman. Emily, busy with her writing, did not campaign for the position, but her friend and neighbor Laura Brown solicited letters on Emily's behalf. Many are in the collection of the Missouri Historical Society in St. Louis, including one from Laura Brown. "We ask your support for our candidate because of her sound Democracy; her intellectual strength, as shown by the fact that she is a writer of note and a speaker always in demand, her service to the party," wrote Brown. "No woman has a wider acquaintance among men and women of national standing."

Emily was elected delegate to the Democratic party in 1921, and just months later, in February 1922, she was appointed vice chairman of the Democratic National Committee. Her job would be to contact committeewomen in each state and develop a network of Democratic Women's Clubs that would, as she said in a report, "do battle for it in political campaigns."

To fulfill the responsibilities of her new post, Emily moved to Washington. Once again, she felt terrible guilt at leaving her family. She managed to meet Harry every month or so—sometimes in Missouri, sometimes in Washington, sometimes on a train or in a hotel. She spent most of the next two years in Washington.

Because the Democratic National Committee had little budget for organizing, much of the work was done through news releases to the media, prepared by Emily's office and mailed to the state committeewomen. The office also prepared brochures on subjects like tariffs, foreign policy, and social welfare. The brochures, which explained difficult concepts in simple, everyday language, were distributed to women's clubs, the League of Women Voters, and other women's organizations.

After two years, Blair's office had distributed 1,170,360 brochures and hundreds of study guides, bulletins, and copies of speeches. With no printing budget, most of the materials were sold at a low cost to cover the expense of production.

Emily had toured twenty-two states and had made two hundred speeches. She had divided the nation into seven regions, each to have its own conference. She had also overseen the creation of twenty-four "Schools of Democracy" to train organizers. Most of the training was done by volunteers. "The truth is that we have undertaken so much that we have overworked ourselves," she wrote in a report. "We cannot keep it up." Eventually, Emily worked with Eleanor Roosevelt and helped organize more than two thousand Democratic Women's Clubs.

Still, change came slowly. "My objective—to organize the women for victory—was not that of these politicians. Theirs was to keep themselves in power," she wrote in her autobiography. A few years later, she told a reporter that women had slipped backward: "Individual women have made successes— large successes—but very little advantage has come to women as a group." She felt that, rather than changing things, women had aligned with men and lost their power.

The challenges of the work increased every year, and Emily depended on Harry to help her handle the stress of meetings, speeches, and campaign travel. In 1925, she returned to Joplin and commuted back to Washington for weeks or months at a time to continue her position.

The children were growing up; both were away at school in the East. Evidently, Emily was suddenly struck with the reality

⟶ To win the right to vote, women had to persuade men to vote for a new amendment to the U.S. Constitution. Many men, however, believed that giving women the vote would diminish men's power. "When you trust us with the care of your children and with the sick and aged, why shouldn't you trust us in this case?" Emily asked in one of her early speeches. "It is really just a matter of housekeeping." Emily Newell Blair is pictured here with her son, Newell, and daughter, Harriet. *Powers Museum, Carthage, Missouri*

that their childhood was slipping away. One morning she announced to Harry that she was going out that very day to buy a house. He answered that "it was all right with him, but I would not find a house to suit me."

Indeed, she found a recently finished. home that she pronounced "unattractive," but she made a list for the builder. He was to restucco the exterior, change the windows, divide a large room into two bedrooms, add bookshelves, widen a door, add more windows, and have it ready for the family in ten days. "I have always rejoiced that I did it in just that way," she wrote.

A month after the move, Emily's mother died on January 21, 1926. Emily wrote that she realized better every year how much her mother had accomplished. "These pioneer women had something in them that gave them an integrated strength, and created a personality," she wrote.

Emily's life had become extremely busy and stressful. Besides her political commitment, she began to earn extra money by writing a regular book review column for *Good Housekeeping* in 1926. With great relief, she resigned from political work after the 1928 convention.

Writing her column required that she read between thirty and fifty books each month, then reread ten or twelve until she could write about them. The work sometimes kept her up all night. After the family went to bed, Emily read until four or five in the morning. She would then sleep until ten or eleven, go to her office, and work until five. Returning home, she would check on the household, take a nap, and spend the evening with the family.

This schedule required that she rent a separate house for her work. She also had quite a bit of hired help. Besides servants who cooked and cleaned, she had a "houseman" who brought meals to her office and attended to her books, unwrapping new parcels from the publishers, and collecting her discarded books for donation to hospitals and libraries. To ensure accuracy in her reviews, her three secretaries checked

⟶ This 1926 portrait of Emily Newell Blair was made when she began writing a regular column for *Good Housekeeping*. After leaving politics, she felt that she was forgotten by her former political friends and later wrote, "It is one thing to want to get out, quite another to find you are ignored." *State Historical Society of Missouri, Columbia*

names, dates, and spelling. Every month, at the last possible minute, she rushed to get the article on the latest train to go to the publisher.

Emily also answered hundreds of letters each month, and she managed to write a book of her own. *Creation of a Home* was published in 1930 and included reprints of her personal stories and motherly advice for Harriet, who had just married. "In this new world the young homemaker has the job of creating a new home. It goes without saying that this new home must meet the needs of this new age; it must take into account the new woman."

Creation of a Home recognizes that each woman will manage things differently and find her own style, which Blair called the "Herself Style." The book advises thrift, budgeting, and running the home like a business. "A new approach to these age-old problems has been made possible by the knowledge of the self that modern psychology has put at our disposal," she wrote. A long chapter discusses the benefits and disadvantages of having children, and Blair concludes that each woman will have to decide this issue for herself. Harriet, deciding the issue for herself, had a daughter, whom she named Emily, on July 24, 1928, and twin girls, Anne and Margreta, on February 27, 1931.

Emily's second book, *A Woman of Courage,* was published in 1931. This fictional work is different from her other writing. A novel, it describes the life of a woman in desperate circumstances who wants to make things better for herself and others. The story, which is somewhat autobiographical and quite sentimental, appeared just as the Great Depression brought misery to American families.

Like other families during the Depression, the Blairs experienced financial problems. Emily reentered politics to work for election of Franklin Delano Roosevelt as president. In 1933, Roosevelt was elected. When he chose his cabinet officials, Emily's hard work was rewarded when Roosevelt appointed Harry Blair as assistant attorney general in the U.S. Department of Justice. By this time, Emily was content to concentrate on her writing and was delighted to return to Washington, D.C.

If she was dispirited by women's lack of progress toward a new era of equality for all, she kept on fighting for her vision until the end. In 1942, as World War II demanded a total American commitment on the fighting fields and at home, she became the chief of the Women's Interest Section of the War Department's Bureau of Public Relations. A few years after taking her new position, however, she suffered a stroke that left her disabled until her death in 1951. She died at home in Alexandria, Virginia.

In her autobiography, Emily said that she had started life as a wife with no ambitions of her own, then took on work that would benefit many others. While she worked for votes for women, she also earned a good income, became a famous writer, and served important roles in politics. Finally, when she was ready to return to a quiet life, she saw women begin to make gains in politics.

As she wrote in her autobiography, "The young woman of today starts free to be and do what she wishes. She does not have the same concessions to make to respectability and the same compromises between domesticity and marriage. . . . Perhaps her problems will be greater, and the difficulties, too, but they will not be the same."

For More Reading

Bridging Two Eras: The Autobiography of Emily Newell Blair, 1877-1951, edited by Virginia Jeans Laas (Columbia: University of Missouri Press, 1999), is the life story that Emily wrote and rewrote. Emily changed its original title, "Middle Westerner: Transcript of a Lucky Life" to "Our Droll Generation" and finally to "Bridging Two Eras." When Virginia Jeans Laas began to bring the pieces together to create a final work, she found twenty archival boxes of pages in the

Western Historical Manuscript Collection in Columbia. Some were written as early as the 1920s but were later revised by Emily; some were worked over by other family members. "There is no original document," Laas wrote, calling the book Blair's "conscious attempt to create a public image of herself . . . a means to present an explanation and justification of her life." Reading the autobiography as Laas has compiled and edited it, we realize that Emily began early to try to balance her sense of duty to family with her desire for achievement and her belief that women could change society.

Virginia J. Laas also wrote the biographical sketch about Emily Newell Blair in Lawrence O. Christensen, William E. Foley, Gary R. Kremer, and Kenneth H. Winn, eds., *Dictionary of Missouri Biography* (Columbia: University of Missouri Press, 1999). This piece summarizes the key accomplishments of Blair's life.

Virginia Laas has written an essay focusing on Blair's activities within the Democratic party during the decade after suffrage was won entitled "Breaking into Politics: Emily Newell Blair and the Democratic Party in the 1920s," in LeeAnn Whites, Mary C. Neth, and Gary R. Kremer, eds., *Women in Missouri History: In Search of Power and Influence* (Columbia: University of Missouri Press, 2004), 219–35.

Cheri Thompson has written an essay about Blair in Mary K. Dains, ed., *Show Me Missouri Women: Selected Biographies* (Kirksville, Mo.: Thomas Jefferson University Press, 1989).

Josephine Baker

She had barely emerged into the world when she
slipped from the doctor's hands. He caught her just
before she hit the floor. Josephine's entire life was
like that. Ups and downs.

—Josephine's sister Margaret Martin

*O*n June 3, 1906, in a hospital on the outskirts of St. Louis,
Frieda Josephine McDonald was born. Her mother, Carrie
McDonald, was unmarried, poor, and working as a laundress.
Carrie lived with her mother, Caroline Cook, and her aunt
Elvara in a dilapidated apartment on Lucas Street in downtown
St. Louis.

The family had been part of the mass migration of former
slaves traveling north from the rural South after slavery ended
in 1865. Elvara's husband fought and died in the Spanish-
American War of 1898; researchers have found no record of
whether Caroline had a husband. By the time Josephine was
born, the household was made up entirely of women.

At the turn of the century, racism prevailed in St. Louis and
throughout the United States. A decade before Josephine was
born, the Supreme Court decided, in *Plessy v. Ferguson,* that
"separate but equal" facilities, like schools and railroad cars,
were acceptable, and businesses all over St. Louis refused to
serve blacks. However, though Josephine would go to a colored school and use colored-only facilities, her skin was so

light that she faced double discrimination. Her family considered her an embarrassing reminder of her mother's involvement with a white man. But to whites, she was dark, too dark
even to share a bathroom.

However, this little girl, who was soon nicknamed Tumpy
for her chubby looks, did not cower in the face of prejudice.
From the beginning, she was creative, talented, and extremely
ambitious. A performer to the core, she would eventually produce hit records, star in movies, and entrance audiences the
world over with her raw sensuality and daring personality.

Josephine intrigued her public by frequently recreating her
identity and background. She wrote five contradictory autobi-
ographies, and several more books have been written about
her. After she died, her husband published *Josephine,* known
as her final autobiography, and in 1993, her adopted son,
Jean-Claude Baker, interviewed performers and family members from St. Louis to Paris, hoping to understand his enigmatic second mother. In between, friends and fans wrote her
story, too, each version a little different.

Josephine never named a father in her memoirs. She might
say he was a prominent Negro lawyer, a Jewish tailor, a Creole
from New Orleans, or a Spanish dancer. For Josephine,
women had always been the ones to provide stability. She
once remarked, "We can never be sure of our fathers, but we
all know we came from our mothers' bodies."

When Josephine was about a year old, Carrie had another
child, Richard Alexander, by an unknown man she did not
marry. A year later, she married a man named Arthur "Weatherbird" Martin and had two more daughters, Margaret and Willie
May. Often unemployed, and unable to afford food for the family, Weatherbird would take the children in his horse-drawn
cart across the Eads Bridge to the east bank of the Mississippi
River where they caught catfish to fry for dinner. The family
also had trouble paying rent and sometimes had to sneak out
before it was due. At times, the whole family shared a bed, with
the children crowded around Carrie and Arthur's feet.

Soulard Market: Some days, Josephine and her siblings went to a farmers' market like Soulard Market to gather spoiled vegetables or those that fell off a truck or wagon. *Art Witman Collection, Western Historical Manuscript Collection–St. Louis*

Though she could not escape her family's poverty, Josephine amused herself with street life in the Chestnut Valley. In *Josephine,* she wrote, "I spent most of my time wandering around the quarter . . . everyone seemed to own an accordion, a banjo, or a harmonica and those without enough money for real instruments made banjos from cheese boxes. We played music that to us was beautiful on everything from clotheslines strung across barrel halves to paper covered cones."

Josephine and her siblings helped the family survive by sneaking into the Soulard Market in the early mornings to steal vegetables fallen from the stands and into the Union Station railroad yards for coal. Josephine's sister Margaret remembered those mornings:

> Armed with one of the coal sacks daddy used to make
> shoes, we'd head to the railroad yard where Josephine
> would jump onto a coal car, agile as a cat. . . . While one
> of us stood guard, the rest of us would gather up the coal
> Josephine threw us to stuff in our sack. She would still
> be tossing down chunks when the train began humming
> and throbbing. Josephine never jumped until the train
> was in motion.

When Josephine was seven, Carrie sent her to live with a family for whom she cleaned, carried coal, chopped wood, and washed dishes. But according to Josephine, "Mistress" beat her mercilessly and made her share a box in the basement with a flea-ridden dog. In an early biography, she recalled that "Mistress" made her kill a chicken she had befriended, which upset her so much that her mother took her back home. In a later account, she wrote that she returned home only after "Mistress" plunged her hands into boiling water. Josephine remembered the spiritual encounter she had as a result:

> Screaming with pain, I fled to the cellar and collapsed.
> . . . As I was sinking into unconsciousness, I suddenly
> saw a light moving toward me. There in the midst of a
> fleecy cloud, God, dressed in white, stood smiling. Lean-
> ing forward, he gently pinned a golden crown to my
> head with a star.

However, when Josephine's brother, Richard, was interviewed, he did not remember anything about boiling water or the murdered chicken.

When Josephine was nine, Carrie sent her to live with a childless couple, the Masons, who treated Josephine like a daughter. Mrs. Mason took her to the theater and gave her supplies to build a stage in the basement, where Josephine performed with a flamboyance that would one day become legendary. She later remembered, "I had a costume, a fitted, tight-waisted dress of Mrs. Mason's, and one of her big hats with a long feather. I felt like a star and danced until my heart's content." But nothing could last forever, and Josephine soon found herself back living with her grandmother and great aunt.

During this time, Josephine was enrolled in Dumas Elementary School at 1413 Lucas Street. She rarely attended and was hotly pursued by truant officers. She found the perfect hiding place in the nooks and crannies of the thousand-seat all-black Booker T. Washington Theatre at Twenty-Third and Market Streets.

The Booker was one of the first theaters in the country built and operated by African Americans. There often were five shows a day, and the same show would run for a week or longer. Josephine noticed which moves, lines, and costumes especially pleased the crowd, and when she returned home, she performed the same steps for her brother and sisters, who often complained, "Every show is the same, Tumpy!"

By the time Josephine was ten, racial tensions had reached a boiling point in the area, particularly across the river in East St. Louis. As America endured World War I, industrial jobs became available to blacks. In a center of industry, the East St. Louis black population had tripled in just ten years, and, according to the historian Elliot Rudwick, the Democratic party accused Republicans of importing blacks to Illinois to gain voters. Labor leaders also protested this "wholesale importation," and realtors blamed falling property values on blacks. Newspapers portrayed them as gun-toting criminals.

In May 1917, the East St. Louis Central Trades and Labor Union protested against the blacks' migration to the mayor and city council. During the meeting, a black man was rumored to have shot a white man, and, as the rumor grew, many said he had also physically assaulted a white woman. The streets swarmed with white men who terrorized every black person in sight. Three days later, a group of white men drove by and shot into some homes in one of East St. Louis's black neighborhoods. When they came a second time, residents returned fire. Moments later, a police squad car was fired upon, and the two detectives inside died.

A reporter who was in the car wrote the next morning that blacks had planned the attack. White mobs formed. Men stopped streetcars, pulled blacks off, and stoned, clubbed, and kicked them, often to death. Mobs chanted, "Burn 'em out!" as blocks of houses were set on fire with terrified residents trapped inside. The *St. Louis Republic* reported on the scene: "A crazed Negro would dash from his burning home, sometimes with a revolver in his hand. Immediately revolvers by the score would be fired. He would zig-zag through alleys between buildings, then a well-directed shot would strike him."

Many white citizens stood by and watched instead of helping the blacks hide or flee. One businessman said, "I have my duties to my stockholders to protect the property and it wouldn't have done any good." Another white woman would not let a black man hide under her house, saying that her chickens would be disturbed. Even the National Guard did little, and some guardsmen may have joined the mobs.

By the time calm was restored, an estimated forty blacks had died, and six hundred were homeless. Josephine wrote and spoke about the riots often. Even though she lived across the river, the massive fires in East St. Louis could be seen for miles, and the fear and grief affected every black person in the region.

When Josephine was thirteen, she married a steelworker named Willie Wells. According to biographer Ean Wood, the young couple lived with the Martins, and reportedly Josephine was happily pregnant until one night when Willie attacked her and she lost her baby. However, Jean-Claude Baker found that Josephine and Willie actually lived in a room on Laton Avenue, and that Josephine had faked the pregnancy. When her period came, a fight ensued and Willie left.

After Willie's departure, Josephine went to work at the Old Chauffeurs Club in the Chestnut Valley, which had employed her before. On Sundays, she would go to the Booker, and she became more and more determined to perform on that stage. The story of how and when she got there depends on who is telling it.

According to Margaret, Josephine was nine, and she and her siblings were watching a vaudeville troop, the Dixie Steppers. In the middle of the show, Josephine announced that she would demand a job from the director. She told him she was fifteen and he hired her. She left town soon after, only telling Margaret that, "becoming famous meant earning lots of money, never being poor again, helping the family. It also meant showing whites what blacks could do, proving we're all God's children."

In an earlier account, however, Josephine said she was thirteen years old and her mother had forced her to live with a middle-aged steelworker she called "Mr. Dad" in return for food and clothing. Josephine ran away, begged the Booker for work, and left St. Louis that same night. Josephine's brother, Richard, remembered, however, that Josephine lived with "Mr. Dad" against her mother's wishes, causing scandal in the neighborhood.

Josephine told another biographer that it was a young Bessie Smith who opened doors for her. When Smith was playing at the Booker, Josephine happened to walk by. She recounted, "Something stopped me dead in my tracks . . . you know, I think it was God telling me to go back there 'cause He wanted to do something with me, and He wanted me to do something for Him."

It is more likely that Josephine was recruited by the young jazz diva *Clara* Smith, who starred in the Dixie Steppers. In her last autobiography, Josephine recalls she was hired as Clara's dresser, for whom she "sewed, brushed costumes, polished shoes, ironed, dressed hair, hooked and unhooked clothes, fastened, buttoned, unbuttoned, unlaced, hung up, laid out, packed, unpacked." Clara also helped Josephine improve her reading and writing and taught her how to behave like a true diva. According to Jean-Claude Baker, Josephine and Clara were "lady lovers," a situation that enraged the director of the Dixie Steppers, Bob Russel.

Once she was onstage with the Dixie Steppers, however,

Josephine proved she was a fine dancer and comic. Josephine's first role, as a topless cupid, charmed audiences. On the first night, she accidentally got caught on the wire that suspended her, struggled to free herself, and was sure she would be fired. Russel, however, told her she was a comic hit, and that she should get intentionally stuck on the wire from then on.

She learned that rolling her eyes and making faces also made people laugh, but Russel would not allow her in the chorus line because her skin was too light. "To the whites I looked like chocolate. To the blacks I looked like a pinky; there was no place I belonged."

On January 30, 1920, the Dixie Steppers caught a night train to Memphis, Tennessee. They could not eat in the dining cars and had trouble finding a place to stay when they arrived. But they managed, and soon they headed to New Orleans, then Chicago. According to a passage in *Josephine,* Baker was fired after New Orleans but secretly followed the troupe:

> Noticing that one of the big shipping crates was unlocked, I cautiously inched back the lid, packed down some dresses and slipped inside . . . I was picked up, dropped, hoisted in the air again . . . pressing my nose against the side of the crate, I gulped for air.

According to this story, when Josephine arrived, she was rescued by a night watchman's family and eventually was rehired. But when Jean-Claude Baker asked the director Bob Russel about the incident, he insisted that he never fired Josephine, as she always stole the show.

In Philadelphia, the Dixie Steppers performed at the Standard Theatre, but another play, *Shuffle Along,* was being staged nearby. With songs by Eubie Blake and Noble Sissle, *Shuffle Along* was the longest musical ever written, directed, and acted entirely by blacks. It was also the first time blacks were permitted to kiss on stage, and, soon, it would be the first all-black show to play on Broadway. Josephine longed to be in *Shuffle Along,* but when she auditioned, her skin color was again an issue. Where her family had rejected her because she was too light, the director would only hire cast members who were much lighter than she. She was told she was "too small, too thin, too dark." But she refused to go back to St. Louis until she became a star, and when the Dixie Steppers' tour was over, she stayed in Philadelphia.

In 1921, while in Philadelphia, Josephine met and married Billy Baker. According to Ean Wood, she met him at a "rent party," where a family had hired a band, people brought food, and everyone paid admission to help the family make money for the landlord. Billy's family owned a popular restaurant, and his father, who knew several accomplished musicians, took Josephine to see *Shuffle Along* in New York City. Soon, she auditioned again and was hired for thirty dollars a week.

Josephine remembered her first performance: "It was as though I had swallowed a shot of gin. The whistles, the shouts, the bravos, the laughter, the hundreds of staring eyes were wonderfully exciting." Sissle and Blake were impressed with Josephine and put her in the show's road company. However, the other chorus girls hated her and called her "monkey" because she was darker than they were. They threw her costumes out of the dressing room until finally she dressed in the bathroom. She remembered later, "I was gradually learning that there was discrimination between blacks as well. . . . Wasn't there any place in the world where color didn't matter?"

Josephine finally did go home to St. Louis with *Shuffle Along,* where, upon visiting her family, she found them crowded into a cold and dingy basement room. After she left, she swore she would improve her family's living situation. Margaret remembered:

> The following month, fifty dollars arrived in the mail; it continued to come regularly for two years. Then . . . the postman brought us one hundred dollars all in one bundle. I still remember daddy and mama sitting up half the

night as they counted out bills . . . soon afterward, the
sum became $200 monthly. We were rich! . . . In 1929,
Josephine sent us enough to buy a comfortable house . . .
but it was fourteen years before we saw her again.

When Josephine was eighteen, Sissle and Blake produced
In Bamville. It had a cast of 125 performers and three live
horses, which ran a staged race on a treadmill. In the show,
Josephine appeared both as a comedian in blackface and as a
vamp in a floor-length gold lamé gown. In 1924, after six
months on the road, the company arrived in New York and
renamed its show *The Chocolate Dandies.* Josephine lived in
Harlem, reveling in her life as a performer and shocking her
neighbors with her many extravagant outfits.

In 1925, a woman named Caroline Dudley Reagan asked
Josephine to travel to Paris and star in an all-black musical
revue called *La Revue Nègre.* Josephine longed to escape
American racism; certain that things would be different in
France, she got her passport and sailed away on an ocean
liner. "I quickly grew accustomed to shipboard life, although
the *Berengaria* flew the American flag and followed the
American practice of confining black passengers to certain
parts of the ship. At least I was sailing towards freedom."

On October 25, 1925, *La Revue Nègre* opened at the Théâtre
des Champs-Elysées. Painters, writers, musicians, and members of Parisian high society all attended. The director of the
theater, André Devin, remembered Josephine's first performance: "As she danced, quivering with intensity, the entire
room felt the raw force of her passion, the excitement of her
rhythm. She was eroticism personified." A reviewer tried to
describe the experience: "This is no woman, no dancer. It's
something as exotic and elusive as music, the embodiment of
all the sounds we know." Another said, "She grimaces, cross-
es her eyes, puffs out her cheeks, wiggles disjointedly, and
finally crawls off the stage stiff-legged, her rump higher than
her head like a young giraffe."

Josephine later recalled, "Driven by dark forces I didn't recognize, I improvised, crazed by the music, the overheated theatre, filled to the bursting point. . . . Each time I leaped, I seemed to touch the sky, and each time I regained earth, it seemed to be mine alone."

After the show, the theater was turned into a huge restaurant, and Josephine sat and dined with white people for the first time in her life. Before she knew it, the best designers in Paris were sending her clothes, and men vied for her attention. One suitor rented her a huge apartment she called her "marble palace," which had a swimming pool. She kept the apartment lively with her pet snakes, monkeys, and birds. But Josephine worked most of the time. After the show every night, she went to Le Rat Mort, a club reportedly owned by the Corsican Mafia, and danced for adoring crowds all night.

In 1926, *La Revue Nègre* traveled to Berlin, where leaflets denounced Josephine, the black performer who dared to perform naked. Even so, her shows sold out. While in Berlin, Josephine secretly signed a contract with Paul Derval, who directed *Les Folies-Bergères,* which had acrobats, elephants, hundreds of cast members, and thirteen composers, including Irving Berlin. Josephine's decision devastated *La Revue Nègre's* cast. Caroline Reagan closed the show now that its star was gone.

In one scandalous dance at *Les Folies-Bergères,* Josephine wore only a skirt of bananas. In another, she was lowered onto the stage in an immense globe covered with flowers, and emerged—again, in only a skirt—and danced the Charleston before the ball closed over her again.

In 1927, Josephine met Pepito Abatino, an Italian count who became her manager. Pepito helped Josephine to learn to sing and hired a countess to teach her proper manners. Soon, they opened a club named Chez Joséphine. The same year, Josephine signed her first movie contract, for *La Sirène des Tropiques:* "I played the part of a West Indian girl named Papitou who longed to come to Paris and was astonished when she couldn't pay her boat fare with beads. A real featherbrain." Josephine was not happy with her role, and she remembered that she cried when she saw the finished film.

In 1931, Josephine starred in *Paris Qui Remue,* which ran during the Exposition Coloniale. The exposition, which covered around five hundred acres, celebrated France's empire, which spanned North Africa, the Middle East, and the West Indies. Its pavilions also showed off the possessions and colonial pasts of Portugal, Italy, Belgium, and the United States. *Paris Qui Remue* was a huge success, and Josephine was voted the Queen of the Exposition. As a black woman who had chosen to live in France, she was the perfect symbol of the sense of community France was trying to convey.

Soon Josephine appeared everywhere, including the theaters, with her new pet cheetah named Chiquita. She also endorsed several products, including a hair pomade called "Le Bakerfix." Now she could afford a chateau in the Paris suburb of Le Vésinet, and she filled it with exotic animals she collected and received as gifts. She had mice, monkeys, birds, a pig named Albert that had greeted guests at Chez Joséphine, and, of course, Chiquita. Josephine would walk down the street with one of her exotic pets, with village children following her.

In 1934, Josephine made a movie called *Zou Zou,* about a Creole laundress who longed to become a performer. Josephine was very proud of the film and considered it to be the most accurate representation of her life thus far. Like Josephine, the character Zou Zou doted on her pets. Josephine remembered: "I'll never forget the scene when I set the bird free. I had hoped to rehearse it again and again, giving a new bird its liberty with each take, but the original bird wouldn't budge from its perch." While making *Zou Zou,* Josephine starred in the musical *La Créole* and in *Princesse Tam Tam,* the story of an Arab urchin turned into a social butterfly by a French nobleman. There was no denying that Josephine had arrived!

The next year, she traveled to the United States to appear in New York's *Ziegfeld's Follies,* and to visit St. Louis, where she bought her brother a truck for his business and visited Dumas

Josephine Baker with Chiquita the cheetah. The towns-people of Le Vésinet were intrigued with Josephine's unique approach to life. One day she might appear in full flight gear, fresh from a flying lesson. Another, she would be driving around in one of the many sports cars given to her by admiring men or she might be seen on a stroll with a cheetah on a leash. *Billy Rose Theatre Collection, The New York Public Library for the Performing Arts, Astor, Lenox and Tilden Foundations*

School, speaking to the children in French and in English. The Booker theater had been torn down many years before, but she visited the site where it once stood.

Josephine wanted badly to become a success in America, and to star in a Hollywood film, but for her, the *Follies* were a disaster. She described her role as "nothing but a body to be exhibited in various stages of undress," and she was shocked that even though she was a big star in France, Americans still treated her as a second-class citizen and hotels refused her. Most Americans had never seen an interracial performance, and her suggestive dances with white men were met with a cold reception.

Later, Josephine confided to Stephen Papich, "I love America, but it seems that when I'm in America, all I have is bad luck. I guess I have to face facts. America just doesn't like me." But at the same time, she blamed Pepito, who returned to Paris without her. A few weeks later, at age thirty-seven, he passed away from an unknown illness. His friends said that he died of a broken heart.

In 1937, Josephine returned to France to star in *En Super Folies* at Casino de Paris. There she met Jean Lion, a rich Jewish industrialist, who showered her with gifts. His family accepted Josephine, and they were very happy to see the two marry. Now she settled contentedly into Le Beau Chene, sharing the home with Jean's enormous family and converting to Judaism.

Jean took Josephine to the southeast of France, where they discovered an abandoned twelfth-century castle, Les Mirandes. Josephine fell in love with it and soon rented it, calling it Les Milandes, as this was easier for her to pronounce. Deeply in love with Jean, she embarked on a "goodbye tour" of Europe and North Africa. But she soon discovered that she was not ready to lead a quiet life, and within a year she divorced Jean, though they remained friends. Josephine would always struggle to find a balance between the idyllic rural lifestyle she enjoyed at Le Vésinet and Les Milandes—where she gardened and played with her animals—and her exciting life as a performer.

JOSÉPHINE BAKER
dans

━━◆━━ As a souvenir from *La Creole,* which Josephine considered her first experience in legitimate theater, performing along-
side "strictly French actors," Josephine autographed this picture
for her mother back in St. Louis. *Excerpted from* Your St. Louis
and Mine *(1937), by Nathan B. Young Jr., courtesy of the Saint
Louis University Archives*

During her travels in Central Europe, Josephine had sometimes experienced racism. In 1925, rowdy elements in Berlin
had protested her visit, and in 1928, Nazis circulated a petition
to stop her show in Vienna and distributed leaflets denounc-
ing her as the "Black Devil." Therefore, the seriousness of the
political situation was not lost on her when Adolf Hitler, who
denounced blacks as "half-apes," was appointed chancellor of
Germany in January 1933. By March 1936, he had sent troops
into the demilitarized area bordering France, and within two
years he invaded Austria, and, later, Czechoslovakia. When he
invaded Poland in 1939, France and Britain had no choice but
to declare war, and on September 3, 1939, World War II began.

The French believed that the Maginot Line, a system of for-
tifications of France's eastern frontier, protected them from
German invasion. Beneath the walls, in interconnected tunnels,
thousands of French soldiers trained and waited. Josephine
went to the line to entertain them, and by the end of October,
she produced a show called *Paris-London* especially for the
troops.

In 1939, France recruited Josephine as an "honorable corre-
spondent." She told her new partner, Jacques Abtey, "France
made me what I am. I am prepared to give her my life." Abtey
posed as Josephine's secretary and Josephine used her political
connections to get sensitive information. She was very close to
the Japanese ambassador to France and had access to Italian
diplomats, since she had supported Mussolini when he dismissed the Italian parliament in 1925. She also knew the pasha
of Marrakesh, Thami El Glaui, and powerful administrators in
Spanish Morocco. Besides, anyone who didn't know Josephine
certainly wanted to meet the famous "Black Pearl of Paris"!
She wrote:

> Being Josephine Baker had definite advantages. Seville,
> Barcelona, Madrid, wherever I went I was swamped with
> invitations. I particularly liked attending diplomatic func-
> tions since the embassies and consulates swarmed with

Ernest Hemingway called Josephine Baker "the most sensational woman anybody ever saw. Or ever will." *Collection of Richard W. Martin, Jr.*

talkative people. Back at my hotel, I carefully recorded everything I had heard. My notes would have been highly compromising had they been discovered, but who would dare search Josephine Baker to the skin?

In 1939, Josephine performed at a great gala at L'Opéra d'Alger. Her ability to lift the spirits of the audience was phenomenal. One naval officer remembered the evening: "Sometime during the show, a list of French artists who were considered collaborators was read aloud. . . . You could feel hatred in the theatre, but when Josephine appeared, everybody stood up. People were crying. She was a symbol." Josephine was not one to disappoint her adoring fans. In fact, just a few hours before she performed, she had driven to a nearby convent with an armful of fabric to be sewn by the nuns there. When during her last number an immense tricolor flag with a cross of Lorraine unfurled, the audience was brought to tears.

In the same year, Josephine filmed her fourth movie, *Fausse Alerte,* performed at the Casino de Paris many nights, starred in a radio show for the troops every Saturday, and worked at a homeless shelter on most nights. German refugees flooded Paris, and Josephine was happy to make beds, serve food, console new arrivals, and record everything she heard. She was so devoted that the French government shared sensitive information with her, even giving her warning when the Germans would occupy Paris. She was able to move Jean and his family to Les Milandes before the Nazis came.

For her next assignment, Josephine toured South America, taking Abtey disguised as her assistant, along with her monkeys, Great Dane, and several birds. Before leaving, they went to the French city of Vichy, where they were given photos, which Josephine pinned under her dress, and information, written in invisible ink on her sheet music.

In 1941, Josephine fled France fearing that the Germans were going to take over the Free Zone. She traveled to

Casablanca, Morocco, where the British set her up as a liaison. She would receive information, take it to Portugal, and forward it to London. Pasha El Glaui gave her his house in the heart of the old city, where she stayed and adopted Arab customs and dress. She wrote, "I'll never forget the cool freshness of that patio, orange trees growing around a fountain. My pets loved it there and I would have been happy had it not been for the war."

Anticipating an invasion of Morocco, Josephine went to Spain to perform. While there, she visited various embassies—learning what she could—and then stopped in Tetuan, using her connections to get Spanish Moroccan passports for Jews entering the Spanish zone from Eastern Europe. Josephine helped many refugees during the war, and she showed her solidarity with them by wearing the yellow Star of David on her coat.

During much of the war, Josephine and Jacques Abtey were lovers, and Josephine wanted badly to have a child with him. She was a woman of many desires, and to become a mother was perhaps her strongest wish. In 1941, after returning from Spain, she visited a doctor in Casablanca and begged him to help her conceive. After undergoing painful and futile treatment, she traveled 350 miles to Marrakesh on bad roads. Soon, she developed peritonitis, an inflammation of the stomach cavity's lining.

Josephine checked into a private clinic in Casablanca. Her condition was precarious, but she and Abtey took advantage of the situation. When diplomats came to pay their respects, she asked questions about German intentions, the Japanese military, and when the Americans might enter the war. Who would refuse the questions of a sick Josephine?

She left the clinic nineteen months later. Many thought she had died, including Langston Hughes, who wrote her obituary. But, in fact, she was well and believed that God had allowed her to live to fight racism, anti-Semitism, and all forms of inequality.

Josephine never accepted pay for her services to France. To raise money for war victims, she even sold a Cross de Lorraine General De Gaulle gave her, donating the three hundred thousand francs it brought. In 1945, she pawned her jewels and mortgaged her apartment building to pay for a show that followed the French First Army through the liberated countries. For the tour, she hired the debonair—and openly gay—conductor Jo Bouillon, who watched in awe as she sang and danced in the cold when the barracks could not hold all of her fans, and when she visited devastated civilians in hospitals:

> I remember her in uniform sitting on the bed of a typhoid victim in a room full of Buchenwald victims too ill to be moved. . . . Tirelessly she sang, talked, comforted, bringing a last spark of light to dimming eyes, helping some to die and others to go on living.

After the war in Europe ended, Abtey found that Josephine had pawned her jewels once again, using the money to gather an enormous amount of meat, vegetables, and coal to help those in need. Today, the International Spy Museum in Washington, D.C., honors Josephine for her work with the Allies in World War II.

On June 3, 1947, Josephine married Jo Bouillon and sold Le Beau Chene to buy Les Milandes, which she wanted to develop into an amusement park. To raise money, she went on a world tour, and on the way back, she stopped in St. Louis to invite her mother, brother, and sister Margaret to live at Les Milandes. Carrie and Margaret went with her, and when they arrived in France, Josephine was starring in *Féeries et Folies,* in which she played many famous women in history, including Eve, the Empress Josephine, and Mary Queen of Scots. Carrie finally saw her daughter perform on the stage.

For the 1949 opening of Les Milandes, over two thousand guests came. Josephine could barely feed them all! There were card games, dancing, drinking, and volleyball. Soon there would be a pool, soccer field, exotic bakery, modern farm, and even a museum tracing her life with life-size figures made of wax. But Josephine had to tour after every tourist season just to pay off her debts to contractors. She traveled to Belgium, Holland, Switzerland, Italy, North Africa, Germany, Spain, and Cuba. When she was refused service at Havana's Hotel Nacional, Fidel Castro gave her a place to stay. In return, she gave two concerts for free to raise money for his socialist party. Later, she would bring her children to visit "Uncle Fidel."

After Havana, Josephine went to the United States to tour, and a Miami nightclub owner, Ned Schuyler, became her manager. He promised to make her famous in America, but Josephine refused to sing for segregated audiences. She was to start the tour at Ned's club, Copa City, but Miami blacks were not allowed in the theater. Josephine would not change her policy, and Ned was finally able to prove that segregation of the club was not required by law in Miami. When Josephine stepped on the stage, she was ecstatic to see blacks and whites in her audience.

Josephine tried to make a difference in the United States, but it was an uphill battle, and she was forced to cancel her appearance in Atlanta after being turned down by three hotels. In 1951, her involvement in fighting racism intensified. In May, a thirty-six-year-old black truck driver from Mississippi named Willie McGee was accused of raping a white woman. He insisted that they had been in a relationship, but the woman testified that McGee had come into her bedroom at night and that she did not cry out for fear of waking her husband and baby in the next room. McGee's attorney argued that no white man had ever been condemned to death for rape in the deep South, while over fifty-one black men had been executed for this offense. But the jury declared him guilty and issued the death sentence.

When McGee was executed, Josephine paid his funeral expenses and paid for his widow to travel the country to speak out against this injustice. Josephine stopped her shows to talk about his death, saying that a part of every African American died with him. In Washington, D.C., she went into a segregated dining room and ordered a drink, but the waiter told her, "We don't serve Negroes at the table." When she hit the stage that night, she ranted, "Here we are in the capital of your country and you wouldn't even serve me a Coca-Cola."

On October 16, 1951, Josephine went to the Stork Club, New York City's most famous nightclub. She was with her friend Bessie Buchanan, who later became the first black woman elected to a state assembly, and other actors. Their food never came. Furious, Josephine complained to the NAACP and to the police, and soon picket lines surrounded the club. Josephine was especially angry that her friend and admirer, the influential Walter Winchell, a white columnist whose celebrity might have rescued her, had not helped them at all. Winchell insisted that he had left before the incident.

Walter Winchell had given Josephine rave reviews for all of her shows in New York. He was insulted to be accused of being a racist, and he retaliated. He dug up a sixteen-year-old news story in which Josephine had praised Mussolini, and he also publicized a passage from her book in which she appeared to be insulting Jews. Josephine issued a statement that she was not anti-Semitic and that she had never been an admirer of Mussolini. Then, she sued Winchell, the Hearst Corporation, and the King Features Corporation for four hundred thousand dollars for defamation of character and damage to earning capacity.

The case was quickly dismissed, but now Josephine looked like a rabble-rouser, and American producers became wary of her. She performed and spoke out against racism in St. Louis and Las Vegas, then traveled throughout Central and South America. In Mexico City, she announced the founding of the World League to End Racism and Anti-Semitism. She supported the cause wholeheartedly. She made similar announcements at other places on her tour, saying that there would be branches all over Latin America to help anyone who was the victim of "restrictive practices." In many of her speeches, she reported discrimination against blacks in the United States and said that the U.S. Justice Department was trying to devise ways to bar her from reentering America.

She was right. In June 1952, Congress passed the McCarran-Walter Act, which imposed new, stiff limitations aimed at barring "dangerous aliens," namely Communists, from entering the United States.

On July 15, while she was still abroad, the McCarran Committee requested that the FBI prepare a special file on Baker for its review. In November, the FBI began compiling another file on her for the Immigration and Naturalization Service (INS) to decide whether to allow Josephine to reenter the country. One FBI-CIA liaison wrote, "She has been associated with several Communist-front groups. She was active in defense of Willie McGee. . . . While in South America, she has made numerous anti-American remarks to the press of that country."

Since the 1951 Stork Club incident, Walter Winchell had been sending the FBI letters and gossip he received about Josephine. The FBI diligently kept track of the letters, along with any articles about her, and put them in Josephine's file, which eventually grew to 359 pages. One letter, sent on October 29, 1951, came from a reader of Winchell's after a 1936 visit to Leningrad:

> I wandered into the Russian bar in the hotel one night of the three I was there and who was the "big shot" of the evening, surrounded by Red Commissars and French Reds, and actually singing and drinking with them to her heart's content, J. B., the only colored person there. . . . If you with your connections, "check up," you will probably find that J. B. is just a highly colored copy, and a poor one at that, of Mati Hari?

The FBI was particularly interested in Josephine's activities in Buenos Aires, where she announced the opening of a World League branch and called for a law against racial discrimination. The American embassy in Buenos Aires recorded her speech and sent it to the FBI for her files. According to the transcript, she said, "I am calling for unity of all the colored people of the world to regain their dignity and their self-confidence. I'm calling on our white brothers to join us in proving to those who believe that the colored race is inferior, that all men are equal, and that there is one race, the human race."

She also denounced the United States for racism, claiming that officials were trying to keep her out of the country, which of course they were. She said, "At this moment in North America I am branded, because I have the courage to speak of the atrocities resulting from race and religious discrimination. I am the traitoress; I am the undesirable. . . . Although it may prevent my entry into their country, they will not stop my activities as long as there are Negroes that need me."

However, the INS could not prove that Josephine had Communist ties and, in 1954, allowed her to return to the United States. Winchell railed against the decision in his *New York Daily News* column, fuming, "How does the U.S. consul in France explain issuing an American visa to anti-American speech maker Josephine Baker? Isn't he acquainted with her rantings against the US in Argentina and elsewhere? Isn't he familiar with the regulations of US immigration? They stopped admitting persons to these shores for being a Nazi, Commie, or Fascist sympathizer."

But Josephine had moved on to an entirely new project. In 1953, she wrote an orphanage in Japan and asked to adopt a two-year-old boy. She got two—one named Yamamoto Akio and another named Kamura, whom she renamed Janot—"A Shinto and a Korean," she proudly pronounced. This was only the beginning. Josephine wanted a "Rainbow Tribe," a child from every race and religion, to build an ideal interethnic, interfaith community at Les Milandes.

The next year, Josephine lectured all over Scandinavia and

In her happiest moments at Les Milandes, Josephine gave all her attention to her adopted children. *Ted Rohde photo, reprinted with permission from the* Stars and Stripes, *a DoD publication (c) 2004 Stars and Stripes*

found her third son, Jari, in Finland. Then she traveled to Colombia, where a woman presented a boy Baker named Luis. Unable to adopt a child from Israel, Josephine adopted a French boy, renamed him Moïse, and converted him to Judaism. She hired a Hebrew tutor to educate him in the Torah. At the same orphanage, she adopted a boy named Philippe and renamed him Alain Jean-Claude. Then she toured Algeria, which was then at war with France for independence, and adopted the only two surviving children of a town whose people had been massacred. She renamed the girl Marianne, decreeing her Catholic, and renamed the boy Brahim, declaring him a Muslim. Soon after, she visited the Ivory Coast, adopting a boy named Koffi. Now there were nine.

Josephine's income could not support her dream of becoming a universal mother. By 1957, with the elaborate operation at Les Milandes and all the children, she was eighty-three million francs in debt. Jo urged her to stop bringing home children, but Josephine simply would not listen. She soon brought Mara from Venezuela and a little girl from Belgium named Anna Bella Rama Castelluccio. Then she adopted a boy and called him Noël. She stopped there, finally, with twelve children.

As soon as Josephine brought a child to Les Milandes, she had to tour to support the growing tribe. But she would always return eventually and shower them with love and affection. Luis remembered, "She had all sorts of wonderful things in her luggage and a heap of packages lay next to her trunks. There were gifts for the entire village distributed at the chateau." Luis also remembered how Josephine passed down her love of animals to the children: "Maman often brought back to the house baby turkeys and young monkeys she thought looked neglected. To our delight, they often ended up in our bedrooms and even the living room. . . . Each of us had his favorite animals, and we had wonderful baptismal ceremonies, following occasionally harrowing births."

Tourists visited Les Milandes by the thousands. The operation was set on six hundred acres and was really a little town, a world village, or "Village du Monde," as Josephine called it. She built upscale guesthouses, cultivated model farms around the gardeners' cottages, restored the church and cemetery, built little huts for visitors, and opened a nightclub and several restaurants overlooking the swimming pool. But soon visitors were saying that Josephine's children were being exploited like animals at a zoo. Josephine tried to explain her goal of "Universal Brotherhood," but not everyone understood. However, Stephen Papich remembered her children as "the most pampered, looked after, educated, played with and cared for children in the entire world."

In 1958, Josephine stayed in the Hotel Scribe in Paris, where she met her thirteenth child, a fourteen-year-old boy named Jean-Claude, who confessed that his father had disappeared and he was far away from home. She replied, "Don't be worried, my little one, you have no father, but from now on, you will have two mothers." She did not see him for several years, but they would one day be reacquainted, and she would live out her final days with him at her side.

In 1960, the U.S. Embassy in Paris advised the FBI that Josephine might soon try to enter the United States. Quickly, before she even applied, the U.S. visa department furnished a complete background history to help the State Department decide whether Josephine could enter the country. She did apply in February of that year, and again the FBI could not establish a connection between Josephine and the Communist party, though she had "lent her support to pro-Negro causes in which the Communists had interests." She was admitted, and on May 25, 1960, she demanded an interview with the FBI. When she met with the federal agents, she vehemently denied that she had ever been a Communist.

At Les Milandes on August 18, 1961, France conferred upon Josephine the Legion of Honor. Friends came to the ceremony, but it was rapidly becoming apparent that Josephine would not be able to hold her ambitious "Village du Monde" together without help. She could no longer pay insurance, her animals and children were going hungry, and her creditors were becoming impatient.

In 1963, while Josephine was performing in Copenhagen, creditors seized Les Milandes. A group of Danish businessmen rescued her, saving Les Milandes, and she promised to follow their business advice. She did not keep this promise, trying instead to rescue the operation by making it more attractive.

In the same year, in the United States, President John F. Kennedy sent Congress a long-awaited civil rights bill, which offered federal protection to African Americans seeking to vote, eat out, shop, and be educated on equal terms. The massive March on Washington was planned to pressure Congress to adopt this bill, and on August 8, 1963, Josephine went to Washington and joined the estimated two hundred thousand civil rights activists, including the celebrities Sammy Davis Jr., Sidney Poitier, Charlton Heston, Burt Lancaster, and Marlon Brando. She cheered the crowds, saying, "You can't put liberty at the tip of the lips and expect people not to drink it." Martin Luther King Jr. wrote to her, saying, "Your deep humanitarian concern and your unswerving devotion to the cause of freedom and human dignity will remain an inspiration to generations yet unborn."

In 1966, Josephine rang in the New Year with Fidel Castro at the first Tri-continental Conference in Havana, Cuba, which included African, Asian, and Latin American delegates who pledged international solidarity. Of course, the FBI kept tabs on her. Her files contain several pages of reports on the conference and recorded speeches, including one in which she said, "This event symbolizes what I have always desired for humanity. The understanding between all continents without prejudices of any sort." But soon, she would return home to witness the demise of her own village of universal brotherhood.

Les Milandes was finally sold on March 3, 1968, but Josephine refused to leave her fairy tale. According to news reports, when the new owner changed the locks, she sneaked back in through a window and barricaded herself inside with her cat for four hours. Josephine's longtime admirer Princess Grace of Monaco rescued her, paying for a villa overlooking the Mediterranean and assuring Josephine that she and the children would never be evicted.

In 1968, Josephine performed in Berlin, where she became reacquainted with her thirteenth child, Jean-Claude. He remembered, "For ten years since our first meeting at the Scribe, I had followed her adventures. I suffered when she lost

Richard Martin, Josephine's nephew, lives in St. Louis and carries on the family tradition by teaching tap dancing to community children. He worked to have a street in St. Louis named for his famous aunt, and she is also memorialized with a star on her hometown's Walk of Fame. Here, Richard Martin assists in the dedication of Josephine Baker's bust in the Missouri State Capitol. *State Historical Society of Missouri, Columbia; used with permission of Richard W. Martin, Jr.*

her house. In my head I talked to her . . . would she even remember me?" She had not forgotten him, and she insisted that he tour with her. Jean-Claude helped organize her big comeback in Berlin, where papers said that the "Black Venus" was back, and at Carnegie Hall, negotiating to get her a show at the Palace in New York.

In 1975, Josephine was getting ready for her Paris run of *Joséphine,* a compilation of all of her shows. She sang tunes from *Shuffle Along, Paris Qui Remue, Paris Mes Amours,* and other shows her audiences loved. On opening night, April 8, the seats were filled with celebrities, including Princess Grace,

Sophia Loren, and Mick Jagger. The reception after the show was huge, and she stayed up most of the night dancing, exhausting her guests and co-performers. The next day, her friends could not rouse her from her nap and found that she had suffered a stroke in her sleep. They rushed her to the Salpetière Hospital.

Josephine died in the hospital on April 12, 1975. The streets of Paris were still covered in posters announcing her show when thousands flocked to attend her funeral. Stephen Papich remembered the day:

> They fired a volley of twenty-one guns and the sound ricocheted in the Place de la Madeleine. It was an honor they reserved for kings and presidents. . . . The soldiers of the Army of France fought for the privilege of bearing her coffin, and they bore it high, as if it were some great shield, and it was.

For More Reading

Josephine, by Josephine Baker and Jo Bouillon, translated from the French by Mariana Fitzpatrick (New York: Paragon House, 1976) is Josephine Baker's last autobiography, posthumously published by Bouillon. It includes many colorful stories that Josephine and her cohorts loved to tell—many of which should be taken with a grain of salt. This book preserves Josephine's unique voice and approach to life beautifully.

Josephine: The Hungry Heart, by Jean-Claude Baker and Chris Chase (New York: Random House, 1993) provides an exhaustive digest of Josephine Baker's life, written by her thirteenth informally adopted son. Baker's painstaking research reveals his own desire to better understand his own enigmatic second mother, and it includes photographs and information from files to which only he enjoyed access. This may be better suited to mature readers, as it focuses on several of Josephine's racy sexual exploits.

The Josephine Baker Story, by Ean Wood (London: Sanctuary House, 2000) is a true page-turner. Wood provides excellent background on the entertainment cultures of St. Louis and Paris, showing the political and cultural significance of the many shows in which Josephine performed.

A fascinating source of information is the Federal Bureau of Investigation file on Josephine Baker (released December 17, 1999, under the Freedom of Information Act). This 359-page file includes correspondences from within the U.S. intelligence community on the activities of Josephine Baker. It is a great read for anyone interested in the inner workings of the FBI. The "famous persons" listing, available at http://foia.fbi.gov/famous.htm, also includes files on Lucille Ball, Eleanor Roosevelt, and Will Rogers, among others.

Discovering African-American St. Louis: A Guide to Historic Sites, by John A. Wright (St. Louis: Missouri Historical Society Press, 1994), is a wonderful resource for anyone interested in reconstructing the history of African Americans in St. Louis by visiting (or simply reading about) city sites that greatly impacted the community. This book provides maps by neighborhood and includes photographs and descriptions of buildings that no longer exist, which is unfortunately the case with most of the sites that relate directly to Josephine Baker.

"Ain't but a Place": An Anthology of African American Writings about St. Louis, edited by Gerald Early (St. Louis: Missouri Historical Society Press, 1998), contains one of Josephine's more creative accounts of the East St. Louis riots, putting herself in the middle of it all. Although she later confessed that she was not in East St. Louis during the riots, her version of events is well worth reading, if only to marvel at her active imagination and empathy for the victims of the riots. The collection also includes writings by Miles Davis and Maya Angelou.

Bess Wallace Truman

She's far more than The Boss. She's everything
in this outfit. . . . She runs the show wherever
she goes.

—Margaret Truman, 1949

S he was born Elizabeth Virginia Wallace, in February 1885,
to a prominent family in the "royal" suburb of Kansas City,
Independence, Missouri. Well-acquainted with every social
convention, every rule, and possessing every mark of status,
young Bessie Wallace was prepared for a life of perfect comfort and stability. But the technological and political develop-
ments at the turn of the century brought rapid change and
upheaval. The world became infinitely more intertwined and
interdependent, and though Bess's life was acutely impacted
by these changes, her approach to life remained that of an earlier time.

Independence, Missouri, was a town of families. It was a
place where a person's last name told a story almost everyone
knew, and reputation counted for a lot. Local families owned
local businesses, but at least one company enjoyed national status. The Waggoner-Gates Milling Company, which Bess's grandfather George Porterfield Gates co-owned, manufactured
"Queen of the Pantry Flour," which was used all over the United
States. The company was a primary employer in Independence
and quite literally nourished the town. Mary Paxton, Bess's best

━━━ Bess's mother, Madge, had grown up the daughter of a wealthy industrialist who gave her everything she wanted. When Bess's father committed suicide, Madge withdrew into helplessness. Margaret Truman wrote that Bess "saw that her mother's way of loving her father, the passive, tender but more or less mindless love of a genteel lady, was a mistake. It failed to share the bruises, the fears, the defeats a man experienced in this world. . . . She rejected absolutely and totally the idea of a woman's sphere and a man's sphere." *Harry S. Truman Library*

friend and next-door neighbor, remembered in 1966, "It's the best biscuit flour in the world. That's why everybody in Independence had good biscuits. It's soft wheat flour."

The 1883 wedding of Bess's parents, Margaret Gates and David Willock Wallace, took place in the substantial house George Gates had expanded and lavishly remodeled at 219 North Delaware Street in Independence. The fourteen-bedroom house was, like the mill, outfitted with every modern convenience, including hot and cold running water. The remodeling attracted much attention on the newspaper society pages, which reported every improvement and cost. The wedding caused a similar stir on the society pages. Madge was called "the queenliest woman Independence ever produced," and David was known as one of the kindest, most handsome men in Independence.

But the marriage was troubled. Though well-liked, David Wallace had little wealth or status, and George Gates doubted that he could support Madge. In fact, George Gates permitted the marriage only after Madge threatened to elope. David's father, former Independence mayor Benjamin Wallace, found a series of minor political appointments for him. For example, he was the deputy recorder of marriage licenses shortly after his father died. Margaret Truman, David's granddaughter, later wrote:

> I doubt that David ever did a day's work at either job . . . but these youthful appointments probably gave David Wallace the illusion that politics was an easy way to make a living. That might have been true if he had remained a bachelor. But few political jobs paid enough to support a wife with Madge Gates's expensive tastes.

Most of the time while Bess was growing up, her life and family seemed perfect. She was pretty and popular, the closest thing Independence had to royalty. Her mother enrolled her in dance classes and taught her manners. Her father held several

Bess as a child. Harry Truman said he fell in love with blond-haired, blue-eyed Bess the first time he saw her. When she refused his first marriage proposal, he wrote her: "I never was fool enough to think that a girl like you could ever care for a fellow like me but I couldn't help telling you how I felt—I have been so afraid you were not even going to let me be your friend. To be even in that class is something." *Harry S. Truman Library*

public offices and was the grand marshal for parades. He treasured Bess and her three younger brothers, indulging them with elaborate fireworks displays on the Fourth of July each year. The family lived in a stylish house on North Delaware a few blocks from Madge's parents. Mary Paxton remembered years later: "It was a Victorian house with a cupola in the front and it was quite an establishment. There was a carriage-house, a stable with a hay loft, then it had a washhouse."

Mary Paxton's mother, Mary Gentry Paxton, was an accomplished poet and led the town's most intellectual study club, but Bess and Mary had little interest in such genteel pursuits. Mary had three younger brothers and one younger sister; Bess had three younger brothers. The children ran around the neighborhood in a pack. When the boys got too rowdy or fought amongst each other, the girls made peace. More than once, the Wallace boys got into a brawl with the Paxton boys and the two girls had to pull them apart. Bess would enforce a truce. Her neighbor Henry Chiles remembered, "They were all afraid of her."

Bess commanded respect in any contest. She whistled louder, spit watermelon seeds farther, and could dominate a baseball game or tennis match. Chiles remembered, "The Wallaces lived next door to the Paxtons, and the Paxtons . . . outweighed the Wallace boys just a little bit. But when the Wallaces were losing, Bess would come over, and she'd decide the battle right then and there."

In high school, Bess was an excellent student and the best female tennis player in town. She and her friends took turns hosting parties and would often end such evenings with rides through town and the surrounding countryside in horse-drawn carriages. She put her dance classes to use at Saturday evening "hops" in local ballrooms and at parties with her friends. Her close friend Margaret Swope held dances in the ballroom of her South Pleasant Street mansion, and Bess would stand with Margaret in the receiving line.

Bess's unique combination of intellect, beauty, athletic talent, and social status made her attractive to potential suitors, and from the time she was very young, a boy named Harry Truman took notice. The Truman family moved to Independence in 1890 because Martha Ellen Truman wanted her son to attend its superior schools. Harry was seven years old. In his memoirs, he recalled, "We made a number of acquaintances, and I became interested in one in particular. She had golden curls and has, to this day, the most beautiful blue eyes."

Bess *(left)* and Mary Paxton. Mary Paxton remembered: "We all had much the same kind of party dresses, mull with silk sashes, colored or striped, and Bess wore what the rest of us did; the difference was that she always looked more stylish than anyone else we knew." *Harry S. Truman Library*

Students in the Independence public schools sat in alphabetical order. Apparently last names ending in U or V were rare, because Bess Wallace sat directly behind Harry Truman year after year. Harry lived about two blocks from Bess, and his cousins, Ethel and Nellie Noland, who were Harry's best friends, lived across the street from her grandparents' house. He spent all the time with Bess that she would allow. He once said, "If I succeeded in carrying her books to school and back home for her, I had a big day."

Bess did not return Harry's interest at first. He was the son of a livestock trader and a Baptist, an unfashionable combination in Independence's rigid social hierarchy. (The Wallaces and the Paxtons attended the Presbyterian church.) As Mary Paxton remembered many years later, "We did not know Baptists or Methodists or Lutherans. As I look back, it was a snobbish little town." To make matters worse, Harry wore eye-glasses and was teased mercilessly about them. Henry Chiles remembered: "Harry didn't play any of the rough games the way Bess did. He was wearing glasses, and he was afraid of breaking them."

But Bess wasn't oblivious to Harry. In her graduating class of forty-two students, Harry was one of only eleven boys. Even in prosperous Independence, most boys went to work rather than attend high school. Harry did both for a few months, until his father told him he should concentrate on his studies. During their school years, Harry would go over to the Noland house, across from Bess's grandparents' house, to visit the Noland sisters. Bess would come over and, though the four insisted that they were meeting to study Latin, Ethel Noland remembered, "He had two foils or rapiers or whatever you call them; and so we would sometimes practice fencing, which we knew absolutely nothing about, but it was fun to try . . . which we did, with a little Latin intermingled."

As Bess was finishing high school, cracks were showing in her parents' perfect facade. Despite holding several political offices, including Jackson County treasurer, Bess's father never could make ends meet. He did not discuss these problems with Madge, and she was far too concerned with appearances to acknowledge her husband's problems. It was probably at her insistence that he had bought the fancy house on North Delaware, which he could not afford, and the family spiraled into debt. When Bess graduated from high school in 1901, she expected to go to college like her friends, but her parents could not afford to send her. She would have to remain in Independence. It was a terrible blow to the family.

The humiliation of being unable to send his only daughter to college and the pressure from his wife and her family destroyed David Wallace. Still working as a minor government official—a U.S. deputy surveyor—he became an alcoholic. His drinking companions would carry him home from bars and leave him on the porch instead of waking him up to face

Madge. The whole town knew of his alcoholism, but Madge would tell the children he had fallen ill or injured himself when he was not able to function. Any illusions Bess and her brothers had about their father were shattered one June morning in 1903. Four days after the Wallace's twentieth wedding anniversary, while the family slept, David awoke at dawn and dressed quietly, as if he were going to work. He took his revolver from the bedside stand and walked down the hall. Standing in the middle of the upstairs bathroom, he placed the muzzle of the gun behind his left ear and pulled the trigger. He left no note. He was forty-three years old. Bess was only eighteen.

Mary Paxton, who had lost her mother to tuberculosis the year before, rushed to Bess's side that morning. "Bessie was walking up and down back of the house with clenched fists, I remember. She wasn't crying. There wasn't anything I could say, but I just walked up and down with her." Madge Wallace never recovered from her husband's suicide. It seemed that the whole town was talking, and the newspapers described the gruesome event down to the smallest detail. Even if the town gossips were less critical of Madge than she would have been of them, she had little reason to expect sympathy and understanding. Being the widow of a man who had taken his own life was perhaps the worst dishonor Madge Wallace could have imagined.

Bess faced an uncertain future. Her mother clearly was not up to the task of raising her three boys of four, eleven, and sixteen years of age. Madge began to withdraw from the world and became even more rigid and unforgiving of those around her. To get away, she took the children to Colorado Springs for a year, where Bess cared for the family full-time and Madge grew more dependent on her. When they returned to Independence, they moved in with Bess's grandparents on North Delaware. All too quickly, Bess had been thrust into adulthood.

People who knew Bess noted that she had an enormous sense of responsibility to her family. They wondered how she could manage three boys and her notoriously difficult mother while maintaining her sense of humor and good nature. She made sacrifices, to be sure, but did not withdraw from life as her mother had. She played sports and rode horses with her friends, organized a bridge club, joined a study group with Mary Paxton, and became active in a number of charitable organizations.

In 1905, Bess decided that she would continue her education at the Barstow School for Girls in Kansas City, a demanding school that could have prepared her for a top college. But it also offered a rigorous supplementary education to women who did not plan to attend college. Since Bess could not leave her mother, this is the route she chose. At Barstow, she studied rhetoric, French, and literature, earning excellent grades. She also impressed everyone with her prowess on the basketball court.

During those years, Bess spent much of her time with Margaret Swope. Margaret had lost her father when she was a small child, but her uncle, Thomas Swope—one of the most prosperous real estate developers in Kansas City—paid for everything the family needed. Indeed, he gave away as much as he could, often remarking that he did not deserve his riches. He donated a tract of land at Twenty-third and Locust Streets in downtown Kansas City for a hospital, and he gave 1,334 acres along the Blue River for the impressive city park that now bears his name. Swope Park is home to the Kansas City Zoo, the Starlight Theatre, golf courses, baseball diamonds, soccer fields, and a fishing lake. Tom Swope cared a great deal for Kansas City and for his family. He would do anything to ensure that his seven nieces and nephews were happy and healthy. But in the end, even he could not protect them from a man by the name of Dr. Bennett Clark Hyde, whom Margaret Swope's oldest sister, Frances, married. Dr. Hyde seems to have had his eye on the Swope fortune, and in 1903 he allegedly poisoned Tom Swope and his cousin, Moss Hunton, with cyanide while pretending to care for them during an illness. Both men died. Then, to make sure the inheritance would not be divided among Frances's siblings, Dr. Hyde allegedly infected them with typhoid fever. Four of the younger Swope children, including Margaret, immediately became ill with violent seizures, but only her brother Chrisman died. Then Dr. Hyde went to New York to meet Margaret's sister, Lucie Lee. She died on the train back to Independence.

Former Mayor James A. Reed prosecuted Dr. Hyde in one of the town's most sensational trials. Hyde was convicted but appealed to the Missouri Supreme Court and was eventually released after three trials. The town gossiped about the Hyde case, just as they had gossiped about David Wallace's suicide. Bess and Margaret's friendship certainly must have been deepened by their personal tragedies.

Another of Bess's friends who was the subject of gossip was Mary Paxton, who had engaged in risky adventures as a journalist, including a walk through Kansas City's seedy red-light district, on which she reported in detail, and a ride in a flying observation post the U.S. Army was testing. After this flight over downtown Kansas City—on what really amounted to a collection of kites—her brother told her: "You have disgraced the family."

Bess's young life and sense of security revolved around strong families like the Swopes, the Paxtons, and her own, but all of these seemed to be falling apart. Certainly, these events affected her deeply, as the community she cherished was dissected in the newspapers and her friends put on trial, if only in the court of public opinion. But Bess was well known for her stoicism in the face of adversity, and if she ever cried or complained during this time, there is no evidence of it now.

Meanwhile, Harry Truman was in Grandview, Missouri, on the family's six-hundred-acre farm, helping his father, John Anderson Truman, try to work his way out of crippling debt that resulted from a string of bad financial decisions. By Harry's 1901 graduation, John Truman had suffered badly from speculating on the failing wheat futures market. The family lost almost everything. They had moved to Kansas City, and John

Truman got a job as a night watchman. Several years later, they moved to a farm in Clinton, Missouri, while Harry stayed behind in Kansas City. In 1910, they lost their entire corn crop to floods and moved back to the Grandview farm.

Harry knew he could not afford college, so instead he worked jobs as varied as Santa Fe Railroad construction time-keeper and National Bank of Commerce clerk. In 1905, while he was working for the bank, he joined the National Guard unit in Kansas City. When John Truman could no longer handle the farm alone, Harry moved back to help, devoting himself completely to this new life.

All the while, he looked for a way to reenter Bess's life. When he finally did, no one was particularly surprised. Harry was visiting the Noland sisters one evening when his aunt gave him the chance he'd been waiting for. It seems that even in her reclusive state, Madge Wallace enjoyed baking pies and cakes for her neighbors, and she had sent one over to the Nolands. Thus there was a pie plate to return; when Harry's aunt mentioned this, Harry accepted the job with what Ethel Noland described as "something approaching the speed of light." When he returned a full two hours later, he said simply, "Well, I saw her." He hardly needed to tell them that he and Bess had sat on her grandparents' front porch catching up on old times. His cousins were probably watching from across the street the whole time.

Harry began to court Bess. The distance between the farm and Bess's home made it difficult—about two hours by horse and buggy and longer by train. Neither method was particularly reliable. The horse and buggy belonged to his father, who could rarely spare them for anything other than business. So Harry usually walked the mile into Grandview to take the train. Both the Kansas City Southern and the St. Louis and San Francisco lines had depots in downtown Independence. The service was spotty, however, and Harry had to take a train into Kansas City and then catch another to Independence. Like the horse and buggy, this could take hours.

Telephone calls to Bess presented other problems. Harry had to first call a central operator and ask the operator to ring Bess's phone. When the Wallaces' phone rang, so did the phones for everyone else in the neighborhood. The early "party line" telephone technology that existed before World War I made it easy for neighborhood busybodies to pick up the phone and listen. They could even choose when to eavesdrop by learning the specific ring assigned to each household. This practice was called "rubbering," and it was common enough that everyone knew it was unwise to discuss private matters on the phone.

So Harry and Bess wrote letters. Sometimes, they wrote several a day. In Harry's letters, he told Bess about the farm, family, finances, and when they might meet again. He was very open with her, an exceedingly patient, persistent young man who generally aimed to make the people around him happy. He once remarked, "When I was growing up, it occurred to me to watch the people around me to find out what they thought and what pleased them most. . . . I used to watch my father and mother closely to learn what I could do to please them, just as I did with my schoolteachers and playmates."

In this regard, Bess's mother was probably the toughest challenge Harry faced. Madge was terrified of losing Bess and did not approve of her associating with a farmer. According to Harry and Bess's schoolteacher Janey Chiles, Madge "was a very, very difficult person, and there wasn't anybody in town she didn't look down on. And Harry Truman was not at that time I believe a very promising prospect."

Bess continued to see Harry, rebelling against her mother and the social conventions her mother cherished. But apparently Bess still had some reservations, because she refused his 1911 marriage proposal. He wrote in response, "I have never met a girl in my life that you were not the first to be compared with her, to see wherein she was lacking and she always was."

Bess allowed the courtship to continue, and being able to impress her was Harry's primary motivation to do well. He wrote after a business failure, "If I thought you cared a little,

I'd double my efforts to amount to something and maybe I would succeed." He told her that as a boy he had yearned for a West Point education only so she "could be the leading lady of the palace or empire or whatever it was I wanted to build." Though not quite a palace or an empire, he built her a grass tennis court on the farm 1911, so that she could "come out Saturday afternoons and play in the shade all the time." In 1913, Bess told him that if she ever married anyone, it would be him: Thus, they were secretly engaged.

While in Grandview, Harry did his best to earn a good reputation. His father, even during his financial troubles, had the respect of neighbors as an honest, hardworking man. When he died in 1914, the schools in Grandview were closed in mourning. Harry endeavored to be regarded in the same way: He worked hard on the farm and was as neat and polite as he could be. In 1909 he organized Grandview's first Masonic lodge. After all, George Washington had taken his oath of office on a Masonic Bible, and every Mason Harry knew seemed to get ahead.

But this was not the case in 1916, when Harry led a zinc mining venture with two brother Masons at a place called Commerce in the northeastern corner of Oklahoma, just over the Missouri border. His mother and his Uncle Harry both advanced him money for the venture, but the mine did not produce. He lost several thousand dollars, much of it his mother's. He wrote to Bess:

> The mine has gone by the board. I have lost out on it
> entirely. . . . If I don't lose all the livestock I have, it will
> only be because I shall turn it over to Mamma. I shall join
> the class who can't sign checks of their own. . . . You
> would do better perhaps if you pitch me into the ash heap
> and pick someone with more sense and ability and not
> such a soft head. My position seems to be that of follow-
> ing a mule up a corn row rather than directing the cen-
> ters of finance.

This news no doubt saddened Bess, but she took comfort in Harry Truman's honesty. Unlike her father, Harry would not hide his shortcomings from her, and he would not quit trying. He continued to work hard on the farm, and only two months after the zinc company collapsed, he tried his luck at drilling for oil. He put in notes equal to five thousand dollars, cosigned by his mother, for what became the Morgan Oil and Refining Company, selling leases for mines in Kansas, Oklahoma, Texas, and Louisiana.

His business partner predicted that if the United States entered the war in Europe, oil demand would skyrocket. But before that could happen, true to the Truman luck, the war absorbed all of the available manpower and investment money for drilling, and the company folded. Worse, they had actually drilled just two hundred feet over a massive oil pool in Oklahoma, which was discovered soon after Harry and his partners quit. If they had only drilled a little deeper, they could have been millionaires.

Harry shared with Bess not only the stories of his business failings but also his fantasies about what he would do with money, if ever any came his way. He joked, "Politics sure is the ruination of many a good man. Between hot air and graft, he usually loses not only his head but also his money and friends as well. Still, if I were real rich, I'd just as soon spend my money buying votes and offices as yachts and autos."

Not rich enough in 1914 to buy yachts, he settled for a car. The hand-built 1911 Stafford was really a gift from his mother. A few months earlier, Harry had stood at her bedside holding a kerosene lamp that provided the only illumination for the doctor performing a risky hernia surgery on her. It was most distressing, he admitted, but he got through it, and so did she. The Stafford made it easier to visit Bess, and he proudly drove her and her brothers and friends around town.

Harry and Bess were six years into their courtship when President Woodrow Wilson announced that the United States would indeed enter the war in Europe. Bess became increasingly involved with her community work, and Harry's terrible luck finally began to change for the better. He volunteered to rejoin the National Guard unit in Kansas City, though at his age he was not required to enlist, and he was busy with the farm and other ventures. But he painted the Stafford red and used it to recruit a new artillery battery. His men elected him first lieutenant, a position that had him instructing recruits on handling horses and digging trenches.

Bess joined a women's auxiliary of his 129th regiment, supporting servicemen like Harry, and served on a committee that entertained visiting soldiers from Leavenworth, Kansas. People noticed that she was not afraid to be close and personal with people. She had experienced pain in her life, and she would listen sympathetically for hours as people told her their sorrows. She also organized and managed bond drives, going door-to-door to ask for subscribers to fund the war. She did well; the district she managed, in Jackson County's Blue Township, raised over $1,780,000 in war loans. Harry wrote to her that her success, "had as much to do with breaking the German morale as our cannon shots, and we owe you as much for an early homecoming as we do the fighters."

During the war, Bess grew very close to Harry's sister, Mary Jane, and his mother. She visited and wrote often and helped Mary Jane get a job with the auxiliary, though it is hard to see how Mary Jane had time for this. Now that Harry was away, it was she who was up at five every morning, seeing to the business of running the Grandview farm with only horse- and mule-powered equipment. She had worked on the farm before and had taken Harry's place when he was away at the zinc mine, but now she took full charge of planting, harvesting, and shipping the wheat to market. She watched for signs of rain and changes in commodity prices, remembering in a 1975 interview:

> We had 300 [acres] in pasture and 300 in cultivation. . . .
> I remember I was a worrier to death. We had a good man,

an honest soul, but he was as slow as Christmas and I
thought I just knew we were going to get the wheat in too
late for it to make a crop. But you know, it turned out the
next summer we had a real good wheat crop.

Mary Jane hired thirty men for threshing time. On top of
managing their work, she and her mother had to house several of them and feed them all.

> Usually you had three or four vegetables and then plenty
> of meat and bread. Sometimes you could get the bakery
> bread and sometimes you couldn't; then you had to make
> biscuits or cornbread or something like that. Then there
> were the machine men; there would be five with a
> machine and they stayed overnight. So you had to have
> breakfast, dinner, and supper for them. . . . We would
> have anywhere from 25 to 30, and we always had com-
> pany besides. We always had a houseful.

While Harry was at the army's Camp Doniphan in Oklahoma,
he ran the regimental canteen, selling cigarettes, shaving supplies, writing paper, and other goods. He enlisted the help of
Sergeant Edward Jacobson, a former clerk at a Kansas City
clothing store, and the men were very successful, even turning
a profit.

On March 29, 1918, Harry set sail for France, carrying three
photographs—one of his mother, one his sister, and one of
Bess, on which she had written, "Dear Harry: May this photo-
graph bring you safely home again from France." Soon after
his arrival at the port in Brest, he was assigned command of a
notoriously rowdy battery of 188 men, mainly Irish immigrants
from Kansas City. The most recent commander in charge of
Battery D had lasted less than sixty days. Harry wrote to Bess
that the men had "been lax in discipline," but he quickly won
their respect. He was older than most of the men and they saw
him as a father figure. They appreciated his frank manner, and

he transformed the battery into one of the regiment's best.

The famed offensive at Meuse-Argonne began on September 26, 1918, at 5:30 in the morning, and was designed to cut off the entire German Second Army. Captain Truman led the 129th Field Artillery behind the American infantry, which was hauling its guns through craters caused by heavy shelling across a mile and a half of no-man's-land before they reached the forests of Argonne. The next morning, Battery D spotted, from a high crest, a German battery getting into formation to fire on the army's Twenty-eighth Division.

Captain Truman's orders were to fire on batteries facing the Thirty-fifth Division, but his men had ended up in the wrong place. He made his decision to disobey orders and readied his men to fire. Their aim was true, and the Twenty-eighth Division was undoubtedly grateful for it.

Weeks later, the German Army finally surrendered, on the eleventh hour of the eleventh day of the eleventh month of 1918. Back in Independence, it was four in the morning, and Bess was awakened—along with everyone else in town—by the sound of church bells. Soon, the sounds of fire sirens, school bells, and honking horns brought everyone into the streets to celebrate. All over America, similar scenes were occurring. The war was finally over. Harry would be in New York by Easter, and he would finally, after eight years of courtship, get to marry Bess.

The two began making plans by mail for their wedding and honeymoon. Harry also wrote about pursuing a political career and the possibility of running for office in Jackson County, or even Congress. The morning after Thanksgiving, though, Bess fell ill with a vicious strain of influenza. It had already devastated Europe, killing more than thirty million people, many more than the war itself. Called "Spanish Flu" or "La Grippe," the virus spread to the United States, where five hundred thousand more died. Independence closed its schools, theaters, and factories in fear of the pandemic, but it continued to spread.

Bess, her brother Frank, and the Noland girls caught it and were sick for weeks. Harry wrote to Bess, "every day nearly someone in my outfit will hear that his mother, sister, or sweetheart is dead. It is heartbreaking almost to think that we are so safe and so well over here and that the ones we'd like to protect more than all the world have been more exposed to death than we." But though they were dragged to the brink of death, Bess, Frank, and the Noland girls all recovered.

On May 3, 1919, the 129th arrived in Kansas City and were greeted by an elated crowd. Captain Truman and the other officers rode on horseback as the men paraded through the streets from Union Station to a huge "Welcome" arch that stood at Eleventh Street. All over town, flags waved and people cheered.

In June, six weeks after Harry arrived home, he and Bess were married at the Trinity Episcopal Church in Independence. After the ceremony, they took to the open road. On their tour, they stopped in Chicago, Detroit, and Port Huron, Michigan, where the weather was perfect and the lake beautiful. Years later, he would simply write "Port Huron" on his letters to remind Bess of this sublimely romantic time.

After the honeymoon, they returned to Independence and moved into Bess's upstairs bedroom in the Gates house. It was not the most romantic arrangement, but Bess and Harry could not afford their own home, and Madge pressured Bess to stay. Bess's youngest brother, Fred, in college at the time, was still living at home, too. Her brothers Frank and George lived in two small bungalows in the backyard with their wives. Madge kept her bedroom next to the first floor parlor, a perfect location for monitoring all of the comings and goings of the house.

As ever, Bess felt responsible for her mother, especially as her mental and physical health deteriorated. Madge was often cruel to Harry, routinely remarking that he was simply not good enough for Bess. But Bess and Harry saw no point to challenging Madge, who was already extremely unhappy and in a fragile state. Instead, they did their best to accommodate her. Neighbor Susan Chiles remarked, "There just didn't seem to be any way in the world to get along with Mrs. Wallace. Bess put up with her, though, stuck with her through thick and thin."

A month before the wedding, Harry opened a haberdashery in downtown Kansas City with his partner from the regimental canteen, Eddie Jacobson. They sold expensive men's clothing and were successful at first. But Harry's luck in business had not improved since the days of zinc mining and oil drilling. In the fall of 1920, wheat prices fell 65 percent from the year before, and farmers all over the Midwest suffered. Suddenly, no one could afford the silk shirts and fancy accessories that Truman and Jacobson sold. The two men closed the haberdashery in 1922. Harry refused to file for bankruptcy and paid off his share of the company's debts over the next fifteen years.

But despite the failed business and the less-than-ideal living situation, 1922 wasn't entirely unlucky for Harry and Bess. That year, Harry met Kansas City's powerful political boss, Thomas J. Pendergast. The Pendergast family had controlled Kansas City for the past three decades. Tom Pendergast's older brother James had founded the infamous Kansas City Democratic machine. Coming to Kansas City in 1876 with nothing, he worked in the industrial neighborhood called West Bottoms until he saved enough money to buy a combination saloon and hotel where factory workers gambled and drank. He bought other bars and hotels and made a fortune. In 1892, Pendergast ran for the First Ward city council seat and won, as he would for the next eighteen years. Pendergast gave jobs and money to the poor in his neighborhood, cementing their support in elections. Then, the "King of the First" ran his own candidates for city and county offices.

Tom Pendergast expanded the family business, starting the Ready-Mixed Company and a number of other construction companies. District judges were administrators, much like county commissioners are today; they oversaw highway construction, payroll, and county contracts, so Boss Tom had a lot

Harry and Bess were married in the afternoon of June 28, 1919. The heat inside the church was so stifling, many of the flowers wilted. *Harry S. Truman Library*

to gain by controlling the judges in Jackson County. Tom's nephew had known Harry Truman during the war and brought his uncle to the haberdashery to meet him. Boss Tom decided that Harry Truman would be perfect as Eastern District judge of Jackson County, and Harry accepted the offer to run.

But Pendergast did not get what he expected. In Truman's campaign speeches, he railed against the mismanagement of county funds and promised that he would fix the county's roads, which had fallen into disrepair during the war, without giving lucrative contracts to political friends. He knew this would be quite a feat. Machine politics were the norm, and it was risky to defy a political boss.

Harry's challenge to the machine rattled Tom Pendergast, but he backed off when he realized that Harry brought legitimacy to his political machine. Truman had the support of the *Independence Examiner,* partially because its editor-in-chief, William Southern, was the father of Bess's sister-in-law May Wallace. Truman was also a veteran with a flawless war record and with a solid Baptist farming background that would bring in the rural vote. His involvement with the Masons certainly did not hurt his chances, and his business failures also endeared him to the public. He was clearly a man who could understand the plight and the concerns of the ordinary person.

In the election of 1922, Truman won (so did all the other Democrats). He soon proved that he had meant it when he said the county would not give away contracts to political allies. Under the new judges, all Pendergast men, the county debt was cut in half, and its credit rating, as well as the roads, improved.

While Harry was in politics, Bess maintained a delicate balance between handling his relations with the public and staying out of the limelight as much as possible. She took his calls, read the mail, and kept track of what needed fixing in the county and which areas seemed most problematic. She learned every social, legal, and political factor that concerned his job and was his top advisor in these matters. She scoured the papers to see how his voting public viewed his activities. But she was sensitive to the fact that some might see her close political relationship with her husband in a negative light. She did not want it to appear that Harry's wife was really making the county's decisions and guarded against this perception, perhaps more than he did.

Bess also avoided making appearances at public events at this time because she was concerned about her health and the health of a future child. She had lost her first two babies, the first in 1920, and a second in 1922. Everyone, including Bess, assumed that the stress of political rallies and other public events had ruined her pregnancies.

While the rigors of being a candidate's wife might have had something to do with it, another factor might have contributed to her miscarriages: the stress of life at 219 North Delaware. It was not easy for Bess to make a comfortable place for herself and her new husband in this tension-filled home. At the Gates House, the Trumans lived with seven of Bess's family members. Her hypochondriac mother expected her to manage every crisis and cure every sickness. Bess was the de facto head of the family, but everyone cowered before and conceded to Madge. Whenever Harry was running for office, Madge would tell him that he would never win and did not deserve to. Guests could hardly walk through the front door without encountering her. When Harry owned the haberdashery with Eddie Jacobson, she would not allow Eddie or his wife to visit. They were Jewish, and to have them in the house would have been a breach of the social code she was obsessed with.

Despite her mother's disapproval, Bess considered the Jacobsons her close friends and had been extremely distressed when they did not invite her to go along when they visited Harry at Fort Leavenworth, where he was on reserve duty. When they took her on another visit, she wrote him that the visit seemed "just a happy dream." Not only had the trip reassured her of the Jacobsons' friendship, but also it allowed her to escape her house and family, if only for a while.

When Bess became pregnant again in 1923, she did every-thing she could to avoid anxiety, excusing herself from any real involvement in her husband's 1924 reelection campaign. Due to conflicts within the Democratic party, Harry lost the election, but the Trumans were ecstatic when their first child was born in February 1924. Bess gave birth to Mary Margaret Truman in an upstairs bedroom and made a bed for her in a bureau draw-er. After the first two miscarriages, she had refused to buy or accept baby furniture, for fear of jinxing the pregnancy.

In a 1983 interview, Margaret remembered that her backyard became the playground for all the neighborhood children. "I had a swing. I had a trapeze. I had a teeter-totter. . . . All nine girls used to come over and play in my yard, and that way my mother never had to worry where I was!" On rainy days, when she could not ride her tricycle outside, she would pedal across the hardwood floors of the Gates house.

In 1927, Harry ran unopposed for presiding judge of Jackson County. The position came with a great deal of authority, and during his two terms he was extremely successful. He paved hundreds of miles of roads and continued to get the voters, not his friends, the best deal possible. He passed a bond measure for a new Kansas City courthouse and another to renovate the Independence courthouse. These projects made him so popu-lar that Pendergast insisted he run for U.S. Senate.

Truman was elected to the Senate in 1934, and the family moved to Washington, D.C. Bess continued to expand her knowledge of political issues, particularly those that affected Missouri voters. She made friends with the other senators' wives and worked for numerous charities. While she relished her time in Washington, she often returned home to care for her mother and family and to escape the pressures of Wash-ington. She and Margaret spent most of their holidays and summers in Independence until they finally moved Madge to Washington to live with them.

On her trips back to Independence, Bess was a tireless polit-ical scout. She read the local newspapers and talked to neighbors to find out what everyday people needed and wanted. She gauged the mood of Harry's voters and sent him newspaper clippings to illustrate the trends she noticed. When a negative editorial about Harry appeared in the *St. Louis Post-Dispatch* in 1934, Bess advised her husband not to accept an apology until after the election. It was not such a bad thing, she reasoned, to have a prominent newspaperman thinking he was in his old friend's debt. Harry, in turn, wrote to Bess about every detail of his job, sometimes several times a day. Even when she was not in Washington, she wanted to know everything.

Bess also kept an eye on Harry's political allies and warned him that Tom Pendergast's power was fading. In 1939, Pendergast pled guilty in federal court to accepting bribes and "cooking the books" of his companies to avoid paying millions in taxes. It was a political disaster. Harry was up for reelection in 1940, and Governor Lloyd Stark announced that he would challenge Harry for his Senate seat. It appeared that Harry might lose, with both the *Independence Examiner* and *Kansas City Star* supporting Stark.

Bess watched the White House for signs of President Roosevelt's preference in the tight race. She was gleeful when Roosevelt dismissed Stark only ten minutes into a meeting with him while Harry had spent two hours with the president just a few days before. She read the *Congressional Record* avidly and analyzed the daily proceedings of Congress for Harry. In Washington and in Missouri, she shook hands with thousands of well-wishers at political rallies, often until her hand ached.

The race remained close. When the Trumans went to bed on the night of the primary election, August 5, early returns showed Stark leading by ten thousand votes. Bess was so despondent that when the campaign manager from St. Louis called to congratulate Harry on his reelection, Bess thought it was a joke. "I don't think that's funny!" she exclaimed, slamming down the telephone.

After that fitful night, she stayed in Missouri to help manage the rest of the campaign. When the St. Louis campaign staff members had a problem with some local politicians, Bess was called to settle the problem. With her help, Harry won easily in November. A couple of years later, a reporter asked how she felt about the experience, and she replied, "It's nice to win."

Bess's daily correspondence from Missouri helped Harry stay accountable to Missouri voters. Washington was full of special interests and the temptation to sell out to them was real and dangerous. But corruption was not an option for Harry Truman. Always with Bess's support, he made his reputation as a man unafraid to take on corporations and lobbyists.

Almost immediately after his 1940 reelection, angry Missourians began sending him letters about war profiteering and waste at Missouri's new army base, Fort Leonard Wood, urging him to look into the matter. When he investigated, he found costly equipment left outside to rust in the rain and hundreds of men collecting pay for no work. Even worse, 90 percent of the defense dollars were going to giant military contractors in the Northeast. Missourians were helping pay for national defense with their taxes, but steel and aluminum manufacturers were making all the money.

Harry talked the situation over with Bess, and she encouraged him to continue with his investigation, even if it meant defying or embarrassing Roosevelt. He took his case to the Senate, which voted unanimously to create the Special Committee to Investigate the National Defense Program, with Senator Truman as chairman.

On December 7, 1941, the Japanese bombed Pearl Harbor. It was Bess who called her husband from Washington to deliver the shocking news. He was staying in the Pennant Hotel— now the Candlelight Lodge Retirement Center—in Columbia, Missouri, and she woke him there. He caught a plane for Washington, and Bess called the airline all night to chart the progress of his plane as it continued eastward through terrible weather. She picked him up from the airport in the pouring rain and drove him to the Capitol in time to hear FDR give his famous speech calling on Congress to declare war.

The hysteria that followed made it even more important that the Senate prevent the defense industry from manipulating the public's fear for profit. Truman spoke regularly on the radio about the work of his committee, and Bess sent him feedback. In a 1942 letter, she wrote that a recent speech he made "was the best radio speech I've ever heard you make. . . . In your 'spare time' it really would be a good idea to take a few speech lessons if you are going to be on the radio from now on. But if you keep on doing as well as you did last night you won't need any."

The Truman Committee, as it was called, saved taxpayers more than fourteen billion dollars. Harry began to receive national attention. *Time Magazine* put him on the cover in 1943 shortly after the committee's achievements had been reported. In 1944, he spoke at the ceremony launching the battleship *USS Missouri,* and nineteen-year-old Margaret christened the ship with a bottle of Missouri champagne. In May of that year, he was named one of the ten most useful officials in Washington, D.C., in a poll for *Look* magazine. His star was rising. He wrote to Bess, "*Business Week* has a big write-up on the committee. Will send it if I can get one. *Life* is getting out a special issue—ain't it awful?"

When Congress announced that it would stay in session year-round due to the international emergency of World War II, Bess moved to Washington permanently to work in Harry's office. She answered his personal mail, edited committee reports and speeches, and handled job seekers. She was paid twenty-four hundred dollars a year, a fairly large sum of money at the time, and more than anyone else on the staff made. It was politically risky. Harry had criticized others for this practice, but he assured the public that she was worth every penny, and she relished the job. They also relished the income. Even at this point in Harry's political career, every extra dollar counted.

In addition to her work for Harry, Bess was very active in the United Service Organization and the Red Cross. She spent hours handing out donuts and coffee to servicemen. She talked to them about their experiences and listened to their worries and dreams. Bess believed that the men running the War Department should meet some of the boys they had sent into war, so she arranged for an assembly of top government and military officials to meet and shake hands with 1,450 wounded war veterans.

In July 1944, Roosevelt chose Truman to run with him as vice president. Bess was not happy with this career move, and Harry resisted the nomination. They knew that FDR's health was deteriorating and that Harry would likely inherit World War II along with the presidency. Harry did not want his Pendergast background used in the campaign, and even more, he did not want Bess to have her father's suicide—which they had kept from Margaret—reexamined in the national press. Bess worried about the effect press coverage might have on her mother, now past eighty. With all these concerns, Bess even held a press conference to express her lack of enthusiasm for his nomination.

But Truman had no choice but to accept the appointment, and in October, Harry, Bess, and Margaret began an official campaign tour in New Orleans. They traveled by rail from town to town, followed by reporters. As expected, Roosevelt and Truman won, and Truman was inaugurated as vice president on January 20, 1945. Just three months later, Roosevelt died. Bess and Margaret were at Harry's side when he heard the news. Now the family would be thrust into a position for which it was not at all prepared.

Roosevelt had been elected four times, more than any president before or since, and it would be difficult for Truman to create his own legacy. When the Trumans arrived at the White House, Bess immediately went upstairs to console Eleanor Roosevelt and to insist that she stay in the White House as long as she needed. When Mrs. Roosevelt moved out of the White House, it took thirty trucks to carry her belongings. The Trumans only needed one to move in.

—•— After FDR died, Bess remarked to her close friend, the federal loan official John Snyder, "This is going to put a terrific load on Harry. Roosevelt has told him nothing." Aside from press conferences and photo opportunities, Roosevelt had little contact with Truman and kept him in the dark about much about the war and other presidential business. Harry was sworn in on April 12, 1945, with Bess and Margaret at his side. *Abbie Rowe, National Park Service, courtesy Harry S. Truman Library*

Bess faced a challenge succeeding Eleanor Roosevelt as First Lady. Eleanor Roosevelt was known for her press conferences, newspaper column, twice-weekly radio show, and many speeches. Bess informed the women reporters assigned to the her that she would not hold press conferences. She was extremely private, refusing to be interviewed, photographed, quoted, or fussed over in any way.

Although she was a reluctant First Lady, she was efficient and hardworking. Much of the First Lady's work was political; she attended daily luncheons and teas. People were surprised that the First Lady remembered the names of their family members and details about their lives after a single meeting. She was so down-to-earth, people had to remind themselves who she was.

Bess was determined not to allow the sheer number of people she knew to compromise the quality of her relationships. She refused to treat people differently just because she was now in the White House. She often remarked that new arrivals to Washington came down with "Potomac Fever," an illness characterized by self-importance and snobbery—an illness she was determined she would never catch.

Bess hired veteran White House social secretary Edith Helm to help plan events, receptions, and visits of distinguished guests. A lifelong student, she hosted a Spanish class for her friends, mainly the wives of other important politicians. Later, she complained that the other wives hardly opened their books.

In 1945, Harry told the *Washington Evening Star,* "I never make a report or deliver a speech without her editing it." Clark Clifford remembered that Bess was a "pillar of strength to her husband" and that she had "better insight than her husband into the quality and trustworthiness of people who had gathered around him." Harry consulted her on every important decision—except one. He gave the order to drop the atomic bomb on Hiroshima without telling her. The new weapon killed hundreds of thousands of Japanese. Its power disturbed Bess, and though she never said so in public, it probably bothered her that her husband had not consulted her on the matter.

In 1948, Harry, Bess, and Margaret were on the campaign trail again. On a thirty-one-thousand-mile, whistle-stop tour of the country, Harry gave 356 speeches. At the end of many of them, he would say, "Howdja like to meet the family?" As the crowd cheered, Bess would walk out from behind a curtain as Harry introduced her as "The Boss." Then Margaret would appear, introduced as "The Boss's Boss." The three would link arms as the train pulled away.

The 1948 election was extremely close. Most newspapers (as well as Madge Wallace, who supported the Republican Thomas E. Dewey) thought Harry would lose. But the Trumans pulled it off. On the night of his victory speech, Bess got hold of an early edition of the *Chicago Tribune* with the headline, "Dewey Defeats Truman." The photo of Truman holding that paper is a memorable one.

Shortly after Truman began his second term, the White House was declared structurally unstable. It would have to be renovated, and for the first three years of Harry's second term the Trumans lived in the Blair-Lee House, the traditional home of the vice president. Their new home did not offer the same security as the White House. It had a five-foot fence and a low hedge surrounding a very narrow yard, and hundreds of people passed by every hour. An expert marksman guarded every door, and much to the First Lady's annoyance, the Secret Service followed her everywhere she went.

Yet Bess was determined to "lose" the Secret Service whenever she could, refusing to live in fear. When the Korean War broke out, she hosted parties for wounded servicemen at the Blair House. The Secret Service protested these events, but Bess insisted that it was important for troop morale that some of the men—if only a hundred at a time—were served food, soda, and beer in the president's home.

Bess exercised enormous political influence during Harry's second term, lobbying him at budget time each year to provide money to fight cancer and other diseases. At her insistence, the annual budget for the National Institute of Health was increased from two million to forty-eight million dollars.

Margaret Truman told a reporter in 1949: "Have you ever noticed father when he's with mother at any sort of public gathering? He's always trying to catch her glance to see if she approved of what he is saying or doing. Whenever she has a chance, she whispers a name he has forgotten or briefs him on the status of someone he ought to know about." That same year, Jonathon Daniels, the former press secretary to President

Bess is rarely pictured smiling, but she was vivacious with her friends and staff behind the scenes. One staff member remembered that "the minute the doors would open and all those people would begin to come in, she would freeze, and she looked like old stone face. Instead of being the outgoing, warm and lovely woman that she had been previously, the huge crowds simply made her sort of pull up into herself." This photo of a more relaxed Bess Truman was taken on a vacation with Harry and Margaret in Key West. *U.S. Navy, courtesy Harry S. Truman Library*

Roosevelt, said, "Bess Truman is a lady unchanged by the White House and determined to remain always what she is."

In 1952, much to Bess's delight, Truman announced that he would not run for another term. They returned to Independence in January 1953. Madge had passed away in 1952, and Harry and Bess purchased the Gates House, at 291 North Delaware, from Bess's brothers that year. It is today called the Truman Home and is a National Historic Site.

After the Trumans moved back to Missouri, their neighbors remarked that Washington had hardly changed them at all. They traveled, visiting Hawaii, Europe, and Margaret in New York City. But mostly, because they needed an income, they concentrated on Harry's memoirs. Bess was the editor for the memoirs and the star fund-raiser for the Truman Library.

Margaret worked for NBC in New York City, and in 1955 she interviewed her parents on live television. In the interview, the former First Lady talked about the adjustment to living back in Independence, where they were such celebrities. "We had a funny experience the other night," she said, "Dad and I went to see your cousin across the street and there were so many out here in front of the house we couldn't come home. We had to spend most of the evening on the front porch all by ourselves because our cousins weren't home."

On December 26, 1972, Harry died of congestive heart failure. He was eighty-eight. Margaret asked her mother to move to New York, but Bess stayed in Independence. There, she helped a number of local political candidates with campaign advice and political endorsements. She still kept track of the news from Washington and Jefferson City. In 1972, she contacted Senator Tom Eagleton, with whom she sympathized after the newspapers published reports of his depression. He asked her to be honorary chair of his campaign committee and soon found that Bess was still a hard worker and had not lost touch with public opinion. Bess was delighted that her cochair on the campaign was Stan "The Man" Musial, one of the greatest baseball players of all time, who had played his entire

Truman Home, Independence, Missouri. When Bess returned to Independence for visits, she refused to allow the Secret Service to accompany her. She wanted her life in Missouri to stay as normal as possible. The entire town was understandably thrilled about her visits, but Bess would not have any fanfare. Once, she entered her living room to meet her old bridge club. Everyone in the room was standing, and she exclaimed, "Now stop it, stop it this instant. Sit down, every darn one of you." *National Park Service photo*

twenty-two-year career with the St. Louis Cardinals. But she usually set her sights a bit closer to home. Senator Eagleton remembered, "She knew every player in the Kansas City Royals starting lineup and had very strong opinions of the plusses and minuses of each one."

Bess also gave her endorsement to what she considered the ideal memorial for her husband—a scholarship fund. Congress raised thirty million dollars to set up the funds for the Truman Scholarships, and each year Bess would read selected applica-

⬥⬥⬥ Bess Truman, 1950. Margaret called her a woman who "never had much patience with the egotism and power plays of the politicians who swirled through her life." At the same time, she cared very much for the well-being of Harry's staff and the servants who populated the White House. When it was hot, or when they had had a long day, she would order them to stop working and take a break, much to their surprise. A woman who worked for Bess in the White House nicely summed up her sense of humor: Bess laughed, she said, "as if she had invented laughter." *Harry S. Truman Library*

tions. Now she had the satisfaction of knowing that young men and women would have an additional avenue into college, which she and her husband had never been able to afford.

Bess's arthritis eventually forced her to use a walker, then a wheelchair. She suffered a stroke that left her unable to communicate in 1981, and she died the next year of the same condition that killed her husband, congestive heart failure. She was ninety-seven.

Bess was buried next to Harry in the courtyard of the Truman Library in Independence, Missouri. Throughout his career, she had done her best to shield her personal life from the public. She insisted that the letters she wrote to Harry be kept private. For years, it was thought that she had burned them all, but a few of those daily notes survived. Only her family has had access to them, except for a brief period in 1998 when Margaret Truman allowed six letters to be displayed at the Truman Library. In those few letters we know about, the voice of an adoring, funny woman is preserved.

In 1922, she wrote to Harry, while he was away at Fort Leavenworth:

> Dear Pettie: It is now 10:20 and I am in bed. There was a big black bug when I turned the sheet down and I had to kill it myself—but that wasn't the first time I had wished for you.

For More Reading

Bess W. Truman, by Margaret Truman (New York: Macmillan Publishing Company, 1986), is a rare, personal portrayal of Bess Truman's life, benefiting from Margaret Truman's access to private files and letters, as well as her intimate relationship with her mother. An accomplished mystery writer, Margaret Truman's masterful depiction of the scandalous Dr. Hyde trial is particularly engaging.

Dear Bess: The Letters from Harry to Bess Truman, 1910–1959, by Robert H. Ferrell (Columbia: University of Missouri Press, 1983), includes more than six hundred letters that Harry Truman wrote to Bess in the course of their courtship and marriage. It provides an excellent record of Truman's love for Bess and his determination to improve his own economic and political standing to prove his worthiness of her.

Truman, by David McCullough (New York: Simon and Schuster, 1992), is the definitive, Pulitzer Prize–winning biography of Harry S. Truman. It contains many accounts of Bess's work on her husband's political campaigns and the advice she provided him while he held office.

Plain Speaking: An Oral Biography of Harry S. Truman, by Merle Miller (New York: Berkeley Publishing, 1973), is a book of interviews that preserve the forthright manner of Harry Truman and of his fellow Missourians, including relatives, former teachers, and friends. They discuss with frankness the social divisions that pervaded Independence society, and how these affected Bess and Harry Truman. Miller describes Bess Truman as "a courteous woman with an enormous sense of personal dignity," but he never got an interview with her.

Index

About the Authors

Margot Ford McMillen is an instructor at Westminster College in Fulton, Missouri. She is the author or coauthor of several books, including *Paris, Tightwad, and Peculiar: Missouri Place Names* (University of Missouri Press).

Heather Roberson is a recent graduate of the University of California–Berkeley and is coauthor, with Margot Ford McMillen, of *Called to Courage: Four Women in Missouri History* (University of Missouri Press).